UNDERSTANDING ANCIENT COINS

UNDERSTANDING
ANCIENT
COINS

AN INTRODUCTION FOR
ARCHAEOLOGISTS
AND HISTORIANS

P.J. Casey

B.T. Batsford Ltd, LONDON

ISBN 0 7134 27426 (cased)
ISBN 0 7134 27434 (limp)

Typeset by Keyspools Ltd, Golborne, Lancs
and printed in Great Britain by
Billings Ltd
Worcester
for the publishers
B.T. Batsford Ltd.
4 Fitzhardinge Street
London W1H 0AH

Casey, P.J.
Understanding coins.
1. coins 2. Archaeology—Methodology
I. Title
930.1′028 CC79.5.C/

Contents

Introduction

An archaeologist was once heard to remark that 'Coins are only well dated pieces of metal'. He was, of course, wrong: coins are not usually well dated nor are they necessarily made of metal. But these small technical points of fact aside, the drift of the comment well reflects the place that coin studies have occupied in the archaeological world. Coins are perceived as dating evidence, as art objects and as a unique species of evidence that is best left to the numismatist and confined to the museum strongroom at the earliest possible moment. It is the purpose of this short book to bring to the attention of archaeologists and historians something of the full potential of coin evidence. If numismatic studies are to transcend the mere identification of coins it will be in collaboration with scholars who need the answers to questions which push the numismatist into areas of speculation which are at the very limits of inference in his specialist field. By the same token the optimistic misuse of coin evidence by archaeologists may be curtailed by the reasoned understanding of the numismatist of the complexities of coin production, circulation and survival. In this work I have tried to bring coin studies out of the closet and expose some of the techniques of study which have been developed in the fields of dating, economic and social studies. In doing so I have deliberately ignored the problem of coin identification. This can be learned, by hard work, from a pile of coins or from study in a coin collection, but not from the pages of a book.

The emphasis throughout this work is on Roman coinage. This is not because this is the only area in which numismatic techniques can be used but because it is the author's own field of research. The same

7

sort of work is being done in other coin series, in other periods and by other workers. However, it is the coinage of Rome which forms the largest component of the archaeological record and it is the classical past which occupies the attention of a very large part of the archaeological profession, so that emphasis on this period may not be entirely out of place. If there is a single thread within this work it is that the study of *processes*, not *things*, should be the concern of the applied numismatist. It is a process which underlies the issue, use and loss of coins. The individual coin is merely the representative of a complex series of events. Furthermore, there can be no understanding of the evidential value of coins in the mass without the recognition that they are an expression of political will and economic forces. What the archaeologist has to deal with, as does the numismatist, is the residual evidence for the operation of these forces filtered through the frequently bizarre behaviour of individuals.

It is a pleasure to record the help that I have received in completing this work. Foremost among those to whom thanks are due is David Sellwood, who not only embarked me on an interest in coins but has, as usual, patiently explained the elementary mathematical concepts which I cannot myself understand. He has also supplied the first do-it-yourself computer programme to be offered to the readers of an archaeological book. The staff of Durham University have contributed enormously: Yvonne Brown drew the figures, Tom Middlemass and Trevor Wood took the photographs. A number of photographs were supplied by the British Museum, and these are acknowledged in the text. The figures for the production of two-pence pieces were supplied by the Royal Mint through the good offices of Graham Dyer. Peter and Joan Scott supplied inspiration and hospitality at crucial moments; and, finally, the staff of the British Museum Department of Coins and Medals and of A.H.Baldwin & Son were, as ever, generous with help and advice.

CHAPTER ONE

The nature of coinage

The study of coins has a long history stretching back almost to the inception of coinage itself. The Greeks, naturally, speculated on the origins of coin and it is to Herodotus that we owe some of the earliest knowledge that we have as to the beginnings of metallic coinage as we know and use it today. The fascination of the world in miniature to be found in the individual coin led to the amassing of coin collections by individuals from the Roman period onwards. Augustus collected Greek coins and a persistent thread of antiquarianism runs through the Roman coinage in the imperial period, which suggests that actual coins of earlier periods were available for reference when needed. Dark Age rulers aped the caesars in their own uncouth coin portraits, setting their mint workers the task of copying the obsolete coinage of the Empire. The Renaissance once more saw the accumulation of great collections of coins and the start of the systematisation of coins into series based upon geographical and chronological principles. It also saw the beginnings of the systematic counterfeiting of ancient coins to supply the expanding demands of collectors, and the city of Padua holds the uncertain honour of having conferred its name on these counterfeits by virtue of the numbers of 'Paduans' that were produced by the skilled die-cutters resident there (*Plate 2 : 1*). With the systematisation of coinage came the need for research to establish an order of issues or to define the place of issue and the authority which created the coins. This work of ordering coins has proceeded to the point where there is hardly a single major coin series which does not have its standard catalogue. It is, thus, fairly easy to investigate the individual coin at the first level of recognition: to find who issued it, when and where. It is not so easy to reconstruct the place which that coin may have played in any economy, to establish what its relationship may have been to other contemporary coins and, most difficult of all, to estimate its possible function as a tool in the elucidation of an archaeological record. Of course, the corpora of coins themselves are something like the archaeological record itself in that they are subject to change as new information becomes available, so that, for instance, the standard work on the coinage of the Roman Empire, *Roman Imperial Coinage*, is already under revision before the completion of the publication of the entire corpus.

The work of the earliest students of coinage was devoted very largely to the coins of Greece and Rome, with great emphasis being placed upon the study of the individual coin as an illustration in a classical education. There was a moralising tendency in this scholarship based upon a romantic melancholy which found an expression in architecture and art as well as learning:

Ambition sigh'd. She found it vain to trust
The faithless Column, and the crumbling Bust,
Huge Moles whose shadow stretched from shore to shore
Their ruins perish'd, and their place no more!
Convinc'd, she now contracts her vast design;
And all her triumphs shrink into a coin.

Pope

Today we have other preoccupations than romance in scholarship, and though art history has its more worldly side, it is the economist who is regarded as the sage of the age. The study of coinage now reflects this view of the world; the economic aspects of coinage now loom very large: patterns of deposit are investigated, social trends are sought and the evidence of inflation is looked for, and found, from the Iron Age onwards. Sophisticated tools of study are now deployed, statistics are compiled, histograms drawn, computers are more and more in evidence, whilst chemical and physical analyses of individual and groups of coins have brought ever more information to the student of coinage. This process is intimidating to the non-specialist, and the hugely enjoyable and relatively simple business of rediscovering the past through the medium of coin studies becomes ever more apparently difficult. All academic disciplines have their own language and their own research procedures, and numismatics is no exception. It suffers, perhaps more than most studies, from the diversity of the material with which it is concerned, the wide temporal and geographical area which it covers and the sheer bulk of the material available for study. Not only is there the already available pool of coinage, institutionalised in museums or private collections, but there is a constant increment to this pool from casual finds, hoards and archaeological excavations. This increment can be very large, hoards comprising many thousands of coins are known and individual archaeological sites may produce many hundreds or, occasionally, thousands of coins. Questions abound – why are there so many coins? What can they tell us about the date of sites that produce them? What historical, social or political information can they yield? These are some of the questions which this book will try to answer.

A work which deals with coins should offer some definition of 'coin'. At once it should be recognised that 'coin' is not a word which is synonymous with 'money', or even with 'currency'. These are three different concepts which make up a financial trinity. Currency is a form of money. A coin is a form of money and may be a piece of currency. Money is normally defined as anything which serves as a medium of exchange and a store of wealth. A multitude of objects and commodities have served as money. Banknotes are money and so, too, have been bars of salt (*Plate 1*), iron bars, people, livestock, stone discs, feathers (*Plate 9*), shells, plates of copper, gold rings and woolly blankets.[1] All of these objects have, at some time or in some place, served as the medium by which goods were traded and status estimated; all have been invested, by social consent, with the essential quality of desirability that is inherent in the concept of money. Coins, then, are simply a form of money which may also serve as currency; or they are a form of currency which may be money. The status of a coin as currency may be only a brief interlude in its existence and even during that interlude the currency of a coin may be circumscribed by place as well as time. French coins are currency in Paris but not in New York, and even in Paris a tourist tendering a coin of Napoleon at the ticket office of the Eiffel Tower would find himself barred from purchasing a ticket to view Paris from its summit. The radius of acceptability of coins and the length of the period of their currency may be circumscribed by a number of factors of which the economic and political may be the most important.

How then should we define 'coin' in itself? Certainly not by externals such as shape, nor even by the material from which it is made because coins have been made of every material from gold to old vellum book covers (*Plate 2 :2*). Nor can they be defined by shape and size. Roundness is only a fairly recent characteristic of coins and even this gives way to multangular shapes as the search for means of differentiating new denominations takes place. In the past coins have taken a variety of forms: round, square and rectangular, in the shape of miniature hoes, looking like knives and, in the case of the Greek city of Olbia on the Black Sea, in the form of little bronze dolphins (*Plate 2 :3*).

The essential defining characteristic of a coin is not its shape or metal, but that it should expressly or implicitly show the authority by which it was issued and which, in the last analysis, guarantees its utility as a means of exchange. This authority may be shown expressly by the inclusion of the name of the issuing ruler, state or city in an inscription on the coin, or implicitly by the use of a design or symbol which can be specifically identified with the issuing authority, like the figure of the Persian king on the coins of the satrapies of his empire, or the owl of Athena on the coinage of Athens. Of course symbols which may have been easily identifiable in the past and specific to an area or people may have lost their meaning to us, so that ascribing a coin to a time and place within very narrow limits will sometimes be very difficult. We must cope, too, with the problem of symbols which became prestigious and were adopted widely and for long periods. For instance, so great was the prestige of Alexander the Great that his head and name appear on coins for two centuries after his death, and subtle analysis of style, collation of find spots and observation of archaeological context has been employed to assign these coins to their true issuers and places of issue (*Plate 2 :5*). More recently the coinage of the Austrian empress Maria Theresia (*Plate 2 :6*) achieved such prestige in the Horn of Africa that her thalers were struck for use in that area until the 1950s by whoever was the dominant political power in the area. There are both Italian and British coins issued in the name of an Austrian ruler dead for two centuries, and the Vienna mint still produces them for collectors and as souvenirs for tourists.

The origins of coinage are fairly obscure and all descriptions of the process by which man established that there could be an agreed unit of exchange between commodities or services tend towards the metaphysical. To use a unit of exchange as a regulating medium between objects which have a day to day utility whilst, perhaps, having none itself is an extraordinary procedure. The equation of metal discs or bits of paper with food, old age insurance and a roof over the head is part of the mental make-up of our society, but the first people to accept this situation took a lot on trust.

The first steps towards a coin-based economy may be difficult to perceive as an abstract concept, but there is a good deal of information available as to when and where the first coins were produced in the west. In about 650 BC the merchants of Lydia and Ionia, in what is now western Turkey, began to strike designs onto one face of the pieces of electrum which, in an unmarked state, had circulated as a currency in the area. They were followed in this by local rulers (*Plate 2 :7*). These areas were culturally dominant and, with the migration of Greeks from the east Mediterranean, the notion of coinage spread throughout the rest of the Mediterranean world. By about 450 BC any community with aspirations to be regarded as a political entity and a member of the civilised community struck coins. From the Black Sea to the mouth of the Rhone a system of coinage was established which facilitated trade and regulated warfare. This coinage was based on silver, but in Italy the traditions of Bronze Age Europe still retained a hold in the areas outside the immediate influence of the Greek cities of the south and Campania. Here metallic bronze – tariffed at a hundred pounds weight of metal as being worth an ox – served as a currency base and it was some centuries before the Italic tribes, of whom the Romans became the most important, gave up the use of the pack animal for the convenience of the purse. But this conservatism had long-term effects on the nature of coinage, since it was in Sicily and southern Italy that the first steps were taken to introduce a base metal element into the currency system with a fixed relationship to gold and silver coins. No doubt this innovation was in response to the local tradition which was used to the existence of a base metal currency system of great antiquity.

The stimulus for the development of coinage has been ascribed to two main causes. Scholars of an older generation, a generation which saw peaceful world empires which drew on the benefits of international trade in an unrestricted manner, have plumped for the needs of trade as being the original stimulus for coinage. They point to the long established trading traditions of the area in which the first coins emerged and the evidence for the use of weighted out amounts of gold being used as an article of exchange as far back as the Assyrian Empire. This school sees the need for networks of traders to evolve a mutually convenient method of transferring wealth between producers, consumers and entrepreneurs. A more unstable age has produced an alternative view, looking to the need for rulers to offer wealth and prestige to maintain political stability and to pay for the services of mercenaries when that stability was threatened. Choosing between these extremes, as though there was a single factor leading to the invention of coinage, is probably unrealistic because, whatever the motives for the issue of coin, as soon as coins are relinquished by the issuers they assume a second function, that of currency, passing from hand to hand in trade and exchange. The volume of the available currency will, however, be controlled by the amount of coin put into circulation by the issuing authority. The concept of the control of the money supply is not new, though in the past the availability of coining metal – gold and silver – had more of a restraining effect on currency supplies than abstract economic principles. The minimum outgoings of a state were the payments to state employees, soldiers, administrators and craftsmen employed on public works. In Athens the striking of coin has been linked to the payment of workers on the city's grandiose building projects, to the payment of jurymen serving in the democratic courts and to the payment of the rowers of the fleet.[2] All of these were people who pursued daily activities, either permanently or temporarily, which prevented them from participating in the subsistence economy of the general population so that they needed cash for the purchase of what they could not produce or have the wherewithal with which to barter. In the Roman coinage there is a clear correlation between the military needs of the state and the production of coinage, with the volume of coin increasing with the enlargement of the army or the increase in military pay standards.

If coinage is so intimately connected with the activities of the state then any information which can be gleaned as to how much coin was issued, and when, will give an insight into the resources of the state, the manner in which they were mobilised and the occasions when calls were made on these resources. The problems of establishing production figures of coins will be dealt with more fully later (*Chapter 7*) and the various methods of estimation without documentary evidence examined. However, it may be observed at this stage that the evidence points towards enormous numbers of coins circulating in the past which are quite unrepresented in the residual amount of that coinage available for study today. Because, until very recently, the world currency pool held large quantities of precious metals, successive issues of coins were produced by melting down their predecessors. We can illustrate the magnitude of the problem by a simple calculation which will be used on a number of occasions, of the cost of the annual pay of the Roman army which in the second century has a strength of about 154,000 first grade troops (legionaries) and an approximately equal number of second grade auxiliaries. The basic pay for this force was about 69,300,000 *denarii* a year, a sum which amounted to some 1,940,400 kilos of silver. Of course the cost was much higher because we have not estimated officers' and N.C.O.s' pay in this model nor the enhanced pay structure of some auxiliary units, especially the cavalry. Nevertheless, the total sum is impressive and gives some shadowy impression of what was part, though perhaps the largest part, of the Roman imperial budget and the amount of bullion needed to keep the coinage afloat.

But the state budget is not the same thing as the amount of coin issued annually: obviously payments can be made in extant rather than newly struck coin and the denominations issued will influence the number of individual coins issued at any one time. We can see something of the relative annual issue volume by looking at the evidence of coin hoards where, in some periods, they reflect the rarity or commonness of coins in circulation. Just such a hoard is that which was found at Reka Devnia, in Bulgaria, the ancient city of Marcianopolis.[3] This hoard of over 100,000 silver coins was buried in the middle of the third century but is composed of many earlier coins from the reign of Nero onwards, with the addition of a few of Mark Antony issued in the first century BC. So large is the hoard that some coins are known today only because they are included in this find. We can, with some justification, claim that from the second century onwards the hoard effectively represents in its composition the relative frequency of coin issues from the Rome mint. Many individual coins cannot be dated to a specific year of production but for the reign of Antoninus Pius this can be done with some accuracy. The resulting picture is instructive (*Figure 1*) because it shows great variation in coins from year to year. Clearly the annual flow of coinage is a variable and one component of this variability must have been the frequent cash gifts, amounting to 800 *denarii* per citizen over the reign, to the people of

15

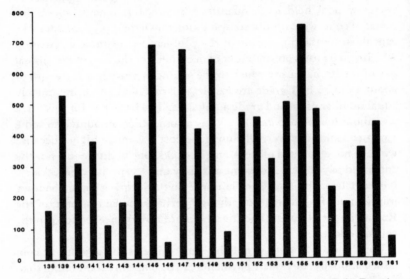

REKA DEVNIA HOARD

Annual Representation of Denarii of Antoninus Pius and Marcus Aurelius Caesar

1. *Denarii* of Antoninus Pius and Marcus Aurelius caesar in the Reka Devnia Hoard.

Rome. Some of these gifts are recorded with precise dates on the coins themselves: the second in 139, the sixth in 150–1, the seventh over the years 152–4 and the ninth in 160. The less precisely dated gifts are the third, given between 140 and 144, the first in 147–8, and the eighth between 157 and 160. If we look at the annual output as represented by the coins in the Reka Devnia hoard we see that the precisely dated years largely coincide with peaks in the coinage and that we can assign the otherwise not closely dated gifts to peaks in the distribution. However, two areas call for comment. The peak for 149 is unexplained unless the coinage for the benefaction of 150/51 was struck in anticipation, as seems to be the case, and the peak for 155 does not coincide with a gift but perhaps represents a heavy expenditure for the war which had been concluded in Britain in this year (*below; Chapter 3*). If the interpretation offered here of the factors which form the pattern of issues in the reign of Antoninus Pius is correct, then the coin issues of a 'normal' expenditure year, that is to say one with no gifts and no abnormal calls on the mint in wartime, were very small indeed.

The implications for this in the use of coins as a dating tool will be discussed below.

We have discussed the issue of coins in sophisticated societies where continuous fiscal transactions form part of the fabric of political life. There are also societies where the use of coinage was even more intermittent and where its economic function may have been less important than its social and ritual functions. Coinage as a ritual tool is still used in Britain in the annual ceremony of the Royal Maundy. In this ceremony a fixed sum, related to the age of the monarch, is distributed in coins which are obsolete in denomination to a selected group of poor citizens. These coins have enormous prestige value and confer upon the recipients honour which is in no way related to the actual intrinsic value of the coins conferred. But coins do not have to be either valueless or outside the normal range of currency to fit into a social ritual. For instance, coin may only be accessible to certain classes of society, such as warriors or high status craftsmen, and hardly permeate down from this level. Such a coinage will be characterised by the high values of the individual currency units which will have served as a store of wealth rather than as a medium for day-to-day exchange, though, as we shall see (p. 46), other interpretations can be offered. Celtic society produced a number of coinages imitative of Greek prototypes in a belt stretching from the Danube to southern Britain. In this area, it has been suggested, the spread of the use of coinage was a factor in the growth of power in the hands of chieftains who rewarded their followers and paid their retainers in gold and silver coins of high intrinsic and denominational value in imitation of the payments made by Greek rulers, especially the Macedonians, to Celtic mercenaries in their employ.[4]

Gift giving played a central role in Celtic social life and we have an account of a Louernios, the king of the Arverni of south central Gaul, distributing gold and silver to his followers by dashing about in his chariot and throwing the precious gifts to his retainers.[5] It is true that our account does not mention coinage in this context, but the principle of gift distribution is the same whether it be uncoined precious metal or coins themselves. In the Roman period large quantities of gold coins found their way into Germany beyond the imperial frontier either as direct subventions to barbarians or carried in the purses of returning natives who had served in the Roman forces in some capacity. Here the prestige of the coins as objects of display and a store of wealth rather than as currency can be seen in their use in jewellery and the imitation of official issues when these were not available.

Such extremes of behaviour as regards coins, from daily transactions as we understand them to elaborate rituals involving the use of coins in a non-currency context, have profound effects on the way that that coin is distributed in the archaeological record. Transaction coinages will be found in a variety of contexts – the market place, the domestic building and in hoards. Prestige coinages, when found at all, will generally be restricted to hoards and to prestige locations, either settlements or religious sites. There is clearly a difference in the manner in which these classes of coin can be used to establish the historical record simply because the former is likely to be more prolific than the latter and the range of techniques of study so much more varied.

What are these techniques of study and how might they vary from site to site and from period to period? The first concern with any archaeological problem is to place it within a time framework, and the use of coins to date sites and strata is a primary objective of numismatics, as the subject pertains to excavation. Coins are the only intrinsically dated objects that most excavations produce; it is true that inscriptions occasionally appear and that documents on wood, papyrus or potsherds do make their appearance, but these are very rare occurrences. In some periods coins comprise the largest single class of metal objects to be recovered from an archaeological site and form the basis of the dating of numerous sites. But establishing chronologies is only the start of the study of coinage in the archaeological field. For instance, zone by zone comparisons are possible in the context of a single site in order to isolate specific areas of coin loss, and presumably coin use, which may be related to the function of the area. This may isolate the function of individual buildings or indicate the economic status of the occupants. Since structures are generally long-lasting, changes in use over the lifetime of the building may be indicated. Taking a church as an example where the value of the coins lost associated with different phases of building varies from time to time, we might, with due caution, suggest that this observation reflects changes in the economic status of the congregation. By extension, a hierarchy of sites may be established over a wider area and the movement of coin between its production centre and its centres of use can be established. This observation may lead to the definition of administrative regions, and the relative size of issues from individual mints can indicate the overall level of economic activity within the area of their supply network. The opening of a mint itself may indicate the discovery of new mineral sources, the relocation of population or some other economic or political event which calls for the provision of currency. In areas where a multiplicity of coinage is available because of the proximity of neighbouring states, the international trade patterns between these states may be traced by the translocation of coinage. An interesting example is the flow of the coinage of the Armoricans of Brittany in the first century BC into the south west of Britain and Wessex, which is evidence for cross-Channel trading, probably through a port at Hengistbury.[6] In more recent times we could point to the large numbers of seventeenth-century Dutch coins which turn up in the Middle East as evidence for the intensity of Levantine trade in that period which the Dutch controlled – a trade shown elsewhere by the appearance of Turkish carpets in Dutch genre paintings of the period.

It is well known that Roman gold coinage flowed into India in the Julio–Claudian period, and the fact that the currency of Ceylon in the fourth and fifth centuries was based upon copies of the coinage of Constantine the Great suggests strongly that trade links, either direct or through middlemen, flourished between Rome and the Indian subcontinent at that period too, though the absence of copies based upon later coinage suggests that this trade came to an abrupt end or that the commodity which brought low value Roman coinage to the area was no longer traded (*Plate 2 :8*).

We may also look to the distribution patterns of coins to elucidate political frontiers and spheres of influence with changes of type, weight or metallic composition indicating movement from one politico-economic sphere to another. The most dramatic instance of this comes with conquest and can be exemplified by the imposition of Roman coinage in Europe and the suppression of the coinage of the Celtic tribes, or the replacement of the coinage of the Byzantine and Persian empires by that of the Arabs. In Britain the extent of pre-Roman tribal territory rests almost entirely upon the evidence of the distribution of tribal coinage, and a political history of this period has been reconstructed based upon the coins, though other explanations for the pattern of this coinage can be advanced.

How are these studies to be undertaken? The *sine qua non* for any numismatic research is the close dating of the individual coin. On this, ultimately, the wider study will be based whether it be a practical or theoretical consideration of an archaeological or historical problem. Dating can be achieved by a number of means. In many series the problem can be resolved, to within acceptable limits, by the information given by the coins themselves. Most coins bear the name of a ruler who has issued them and some rulers even issue coins with their regnal dates upon them in either a direct or indirect form. Others issued coins to celebrate events dated by other sources, such as historical documents or inscriptions, and since the sixteenth century most coinage has borne the actual year of its emission. But even coins with rulers' names, or those of magistrates, can present problems; some long-reigning Roman emperors or Persian monarchs, for instance, have coinages whose issue dates cannot be determined to within better than a ten year span. But for all practical purposes these are acceptable limits.

As examples of methodology let us briefly examine a couple of extreme examples of the problems of establishing a coin date sequence in a series: the coinage of the Parthian Empire and the Axumite kingdom.

The creation of a non-Greek ruling house in what had been Persia, until the conquest of Alexander the Great, was the work of one Arsaces who broke away from the Seleucid kingdom in 247 BC. The empire which he founded survived, after a further period of Seleucid control, until it was brought down in AD 224 by Ardashir, who claimed to be restoring the ancient Persian monarchy of Darius and Xerxes and who initiated the Sassanian period of Iranian history. Over nearly five centuries some forty kings ruled the Parthian state. These kings struck an abundant silver coinage but the coins have almost unvarying reverse types and legends; only very rarely do they bear any obverse legend. To make matters worse, for constitutional reasons all Parthian kings took their throne name from the founder of the dynasty, yet no king, after the first two, actually bore the name Arsaces in his own right and no ancient authority refers to these kings except by their real personal names. So we have forty kings, all called Arsaces on the coins, and the problem is to attach the right coinage to right historical personality (*Plate 2 : 9*).

There are a few fixed points. Firstly, a very few personal names appear on large denomination silver coins and the portraits can be identified with those on the more prolific standard denomination, the drachm. Then there is a perceptible change from a Hellenistic style of portraiture to an Iranian style, and there is the evidence of boards wherein the frequency of issues can be observed varying in proportion according to the date of burial and in which the state of wear of the coins composing the hoards can be used to establish an internal chronology. Overlapping hoards allow a sequence of issues to be established and this, with the occasional use of a regnal date on the coins, permits a chronology to be built up which can be fitted to the narrative evidence of Roman historians. Coins have been found in archaeological deposits which can be dated by other than numismatic means. Our sources tell us something of the length of reign of individual kings so that scarcer coins can be attributed to shorter reigns and abundant coins to the longer. Finally, the study of the coins themselves reveals a continuity of craftsmanship in the preparation of the dies from which the coins are struck which spans more than one reign, so that the distinctive 'signature' of the individual craftsman can be recognised. Resolution of all the problems of this coinage has not been achieved and reattributions are made from time to time but, on the whole, the pattern of the coinage of the countervailing power to Rome has been established, despite its inherent problems.[7]

Our second example lacks the mass of coinage which is available from the Parthians so that a different technique was required to elucidate its chronological problems. The technique was nearly as old as the coinage itself. The kingdom of Axum was situated on the lower reaches of the Nile and flourished between the first and seventh centuries AD. Only two fixed points existed in this coinage, that a king named Ezanas reigned in AD 356 and was converted to Christianity and that another king, Khaleb, was on the throne in c.AD 525 and led an expedition to conquer the Himyarite kingdom of southern Arabia. Twelve rulers are named on the gold coinage of the Axumite kingdom and the arrangement of their reigns has been based upon stylistic criteria. It has been observed, however, that there is a gradual debasement of the Axumite gold coinage, a debasement in both the fineness of the gold employed in the coinage and in the weight of the coins themselves. Axumite gold coins are far too rare and expensive to be subjected to destructive analysis but, by specific gravity tests, resorting to Archimedes' principle, it is possible to establish the gold content of the coins. The content falls in regular stages, and it can be reasonably postulated that successive rulers changed the composition of the coins. Given this, it is possible to establish an order of issue which corresponds with the relative position of the issuer in the list of Axumite kings. Of course, this is a relative date, with a floating chronology, since the length of reigns or the regnal dates of the individual kings cannot be established by purely numismatic methods.[8]

Not all coin series are as difficult as these to elucidate but many are, and, as the questions which are asked by scholars become more specific, so the quest for precision intensifies. It can be a disenchantment to scholars who are not numismatists and who attempt to use coin evidence, when they find that a dense thicket of chronological research has to be penetrated before they can have access to what, in the end, may be a simple piece of information. The fact that the silver pennies issued during the long reign of Edward I (1272–1307) can be divided into no less than ten classes and 34 subclasses, or that the Short Cross coinage struck in the name of Henry II (1154–1189) can be divided into eight classes may seem irrelevant to the historian. But each of the classes has a chronological significance and it is as well to know that, the name on the coin notwithstanding, Henry II Classes Two and Three were struck by Richard I, Classes Four and Five by King John and Classes Six to Eight by Henry III.[9]

But one should not be dissuaded from attempting to use coins as a tool of historical and archaeological research simply because the language and literature of numismatics looks obscure and technical. Coins are an integral part of the historical record. Many are primary documents in their own right, the sole surviving record of events and, at the very least, a tangible connection with the past which attaches the modern coin-user to his predecessor over two and a half millennia of continuous monetary experience.

CHAPTER TWO

The iconography of coinage

If the original intention in placing a design on a coin was to validate it by reference to the power or integrity of the issuer, it was not long before those issuers used the coin as a medium for enhancing their status and for conveying a view of their policies and achievements to the users of their coinage. This propagandist use of coinage developed in the issues of the Hellenistic rulers who succeeded Alexander the Great but came to a climax in the issues of the Roman imperial period. Since then propagandist coinage has been issued by almost all states in one form or other and the theme persists through to our own day. Typical of the later development of this use of coinage is the so-called 'Declaration' coinage of Charles the First which proclaimed that Charles followed a policy which enshrined support for the Protestant religion, the laws of England and the liberty of Parliament (*Plate 3:1*). That his policies were, in the view of many of his subjects, entirely contrary to this declaration was made clear on the battlefields of the Civil War and acts as a reminder that what a coin purports to tell us may be far removed from the empirical truth or the truth as perceived by the recipients of the coinage. It is of course a further irony that the victorious Parliament continued to issue coin in Charles' name, proclaiming his divine right to rule, up to the moment of his execution.

Naturally it is a matter of keen academic dispute as to precisely what credence may be given to coins as historical documents when we lack any other corroborative source of information. There is an even greater problem when the coin interpreted is an iconographic type without overt inscriptional evidence, such as that cited for the coinage of Charles I. There is no limit to the uncontrolled speculation which the interpretation of coin types allows. We may speculate, as some future scholar might, upon the themes presented by British coins. The 5-pence piece displays a large Scottish thistle. Is this a reflection of the importance of Scottish nationalism as a political force in the 1960s? If it is, what then of the equally strong Welsh national sentiment? Of course, the 2-pence piece with the Prince of Wales' feathers clearly reflects the equal importance of Celtic nationalism. But does it? Surviving contemporary documents demonstrate that in the 1960s and 70s there was an almost hysterical interest in the marital prospects of the heir to the throne – is this what is reflected in the coinage and not the political problem? This is hardly an exaggeration of the position which numismatists have adopted in their handling of the interpretation of coins, but there is, as we shall see, a legitimate and fruitful use for the study of coins either individually or in the mass to illuminate political and economic questions from iconographic studies.

Our age does not consciously associate symbolism with daily life, though symbols abound around us pointing to bus-stops, adorning petrol stations or worn as clothing by the young, the clergy, the military and others in society whose outward appearance is a symbolic reference to their function or status. There may be a reluctance to accept that elaborate and subtle symbolism played an important place in society in the past. However, when the emperor Justinian II (685–695) was restored to the throne he sat in state with his feet placed upon the necks of his two rivals, Leontius and Tiberius Apsimarus, in conscious emulation of the account of the Second Coming, in which Christ would tread down the lion (Leontius) and the serpent (Apsimarus). The symbolism was certainly not lost upon his subjects.

We can examine some of the areas in which symbolism impinges on coin. The most obvious symbolic use in coinage is found in the fossilisation of the features of the ruler. On his coinage the emperor Augustus remained the youthful victor of Actium throughout his life, whilst, upon his accession, the emperor Domitian underwent a miraculous transformation from a heavy, plain featured prince to an imperious Adonis. Queen Victoria remained a teenager between her accession in 1837 and her jubilee, celebrated in 1887. Only then did her coinage record the passage from extreme youth to mature old age, and Elizabeth II has only recently achieved a mature portrait. Simple flattery is not necessarily the reason for preserving the features of the ruler in a time-warp – the nature of coin as money is a consideration. Frequent changes of style and appearance may be associated, for right or wrong reasons, with changes in value so that user and consumer confidence may be sapped. Equally important are the social values of stability and order represented by fossilisation and this may be enhanced by the use of religious symbolism in conjunction with the features of the ruler. To this end the ruler may take on some of the trappings of divinity, his head may display the sun-rays of Apollo (*Plate 3:2*) or his hand may grasp the club of Hercules (*Plate 3:3*). The hand of God may hover over the ruler's head in benediction (*Plate 3:4, 6*), or the saints and angels accompany his effigy to confirm divine approval of the reign (*Plate 3:5*). The features of the ruler may themselves become divine, as in the late Roman empire, so that tampering with the coinage becomes an act of sacrilege, and thus the sanction of religion is used to support an unsound currency system.

Symbolism may not, however, always be interpreted as the devisors intended. The notorious case of the crown piece issued to commemorate Britain's entry into the European Common Market may be cited. This coin depicts the hands of the nine members of the EEC clasped in friendship, but the popular interpretation is somewhat different and suggests that the symbolism shows each member trying to stop a greedy fellow member's hand getting into the Community till (*Plate 4:1*). A more serious misinterpretation of numismatic symbolism occurred in the early years of the Byzantine empire. The gold coinage of the emperor Justin II (565–578) depicted the emperor in full of military dress holding a figure of Victory. Such an apparently innocuous use of one of the old symbols of Roman power induced the Christian populace of Constantinople to street riots, and their fury was only controlled when the patriarch persuaded them that the figure of Victory was an angel whispering divine advice into the imperial ear (*Plate 4:2*).

A fruitful area of research lies in the identification of lost works of art and vanished buildings from their representation on coins,[1] but these representations are themselves subject to conventionalisation or symbolic representation. Happily a number of buildings survive, such as Trajan's Column, the Flavian Colosseum, the temple complex at Baalbek and the Parthenon, which are the subject of treatment as coin types and from which we can estimate the amount of schematisation involved in the presentation of buildings on coins in antiquity. A degree of simplification must always be employed when a complex structure or work of art is placed within the narrow confines of a coin, and a series of conventions may be established which aims at presenting to the viewer the essence of the object rather than its totality. In the case of buildings the viewer may be presented only with the elements of the architecture which struck contemporaries as notable and these elements may not be those that we would regard as the most important.

About 800 different ancient buildings now entirely lost or reduced to rubble are represented on Greek and Roman coins, providing an incomparable archive of architectural history; whilst European coins and medals of the sixteenth to nineteenth centuries are a still untapped source of art and architectural information.

Let us look at a number of examples of both extant and long vanished buildings. One of the commonest architectural coins is that issued by Nero to celebrate the opening of a new market place in Rome (*Plate 4:3*). In fact the *macellum* was more like a hypermarket than anything else and figures largely in Nero's propagandist coinage. The coin itself, a brass *dupondius,* the denomination most widely used in small market transactions at the time, depicts only an interior corner of the large multi-storied and porticoed market together with an elaborate domed kiosk which stood in the centre of the whole complex. The kiosk represented the popular image of the whole (*Figure 2*) just as Nelson's Column in London can represent the whole complex of buildings around Trafalgar Square.[2] Clearly artists sought to bring to the spectator only the most important elements of a structure, especially if the coins were struck for very local circulation and the buildings depicted were very familiar from daily contact.

In the case of religious buildings specific rules were evolved so that the most important element of the building, the cult statue itself, appeared in a primary position in the composition. Consequently the god, or gods, would appear apparently outside the building which they inhabited. In fact an observer in antiquity would understand that what the numismatic artist was presenting was a view of the temple which was, simultaneously, a view of the exterior and interior of the building. To accommodate this convention the columns of a temple's portico may be rearranged so that the cult figure occupies a central place in the facade of the structure. To this end, for instance, an octostyle

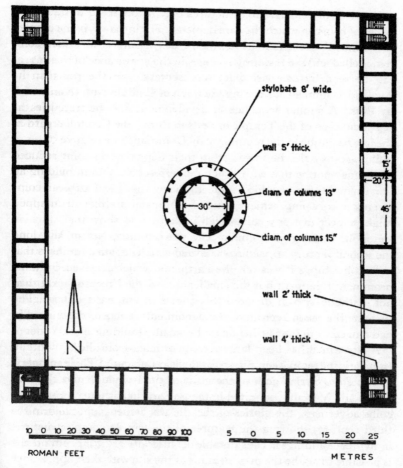

2. The Macellum of Nero, groundplan (after Rainbird, 1971).

structure, which in reality had the eight columns of its facade regularly placed at equal intervals, might be represented as having two sets of four columns with a wide central opening in which the cult figure makes its appearance (*Plate 4:4*). A further convention adds an architectural element from the interior of the temple to the representation of the exterior when the arched niche in which the cult statue stands is projected into the triangular pediment of the facade, giving the appearance of an arcuated facade (*Plate 4:5*).

27

Occasionally changes to structures may be observed in successive issues of coins on which they are depicted. For instance, in the reign of Antoninus Pius the famous lighthouse at Alexandria was extensively remodelled and the resulting changes in the appearance of the Pharos can be seen by comparing its representation on the coins of the Alexandria mint struck during the reign of Hadrian with those struck by Pius.[3] A similar sequence of development may be traced in the representation of the Temple of Zeus in Rome, the Capitoleum, from the late Republic to the rebuilding by Domitian. The relative status of buildings may also be traced from their depiction on coins and this status may not be that with which modern scholarship imbues them. For example, few would dispute the view that the Parthenon represents a crowning achievement of European architecture and we might expect that any coin which undertook to show the Athenian Acropolis would give prominence to this building. Not so. When, in the second century AD, a coin was issued which depicted the Acropolis and its buildings it was not the Parthenon which received the most prominent treatment but the smaller shrine, the Erechtheum. It was not aesthetics which dictated this choice of emphasis but religion, since by the second century AD the main cult centre of the Acropolis had moved from the Parthenon to the smaller building.

A site which has been largely reconstructed from the evidence of coinage is the temple complex at Baalbek in Lebanon.[4] This sanctuary, dedicated to Syrian gods in the guise of the Roman deities, Jupiter, Venus and Mercury, acquired immense fame in antiquity. A series of coins advertising the glories of the site was issued, especially in the third century, showing the features of the temple complex and the individual buildings in considerable detail (*Plate 4 :6, 7*). From these it is possible to clothe the present ruins of the site with their appearance in their heyday and demonstrate the occurrence of strictly local building traits being employed in buildings which, in the surviving ground plans, are entirely classical in form. To take an example, coins show that the Temple of Jupiter departed from the canons of classical style by the employment of a large window in the tympanum above the columns of the facade. This area would normally be reserved for the display of a group of heroic statuary, but in Syrian architecture the need to light the interior sanctuary for ritual purposes dictated the insertion of an opening into an architectural setting which was not designed to receive it.

Such examples need not be restricted to ancient coins. With the revival of pictorial values in Europe from the late Middle Ages we once again enter a world in which realistic portraiture became important and major monuments feature on the coinage and on privately issued medals and tokens. In the latter field, England in the seventeenth and eighteenth centuries offers an incomparable visual record of the growth of commerce and the progress of the Industrial Revolution with ships, mills, machinery and industrial processes widely illustrated.

We may extend the use of coinage as a visual record of the past into the field of portraiture where we have a sequence of images of the men and women around whom some of the great events of history have revolved. Whether these individuals actually controlled events is another question. Romanticising historians once sought to trace, *ex post facto*, the actions of men in their features. Few would follow this imaginative historical method today. Actions are dictated by unimpeded social processes, according to current general historical theory; but then current historical theory is itself an unimpeded imaginative process.

Yet the manner in which rulers and politicians choose to have themselves portrayed may have little to do with general historical theory and very much to do with the more personal conception of 'greatness', or some other esteemed quality. To this end, as we have seen, a number of conventions have evolved in numismatic art which are designed to convey to the spectator the power, sagacity, benevolence, and so forth, of the ruler. That this was an important concept, and indeed remains so to this day, can be seen from the actions of rival factions in the Roman world who used the image on the coinage as a surrogate for the person depicted.

The concept of *damnatio memoriae* was reserved in Roman law for the extinction of the memory of those whom, in their lifetime, the state had been unable to control. This effectively meant emperors whose actions were more than usually inimical to the interests of the senatorial order, but whom these same senators had treated with awed deference in their lifetime. The list of emperors subjected to *damnatio* is long, because usurpers were automatically included in this category, and by the third century the declaration of damnation was at the behest of the emperor himself rather than an initiative of the Senate. The extinction of the memory of the deceased, the creation of a non-person, is not unknown in recent political history in Eastern Europe and the modern practice has much in common with the Roman tradition. With the act of damnation all laws passed by the deceased, unless otherwise specified, fell into abeyance, all statues were destroyed, painted likenesses were defaced, and the name of the condemned was carefully cut away from his inscriptions where it occurred with uncondemned colleagues, or the inscriptions themselves were destroyed. The treatment of the coinage followed the same lines. We know that the coinage of Caligula was melted down, as was that of Geta, the brother of Caracalla. Individual coins might have the offending features erased (*Plate 5 : 1, 2, 3*) or the offending name expunged. The result of this action on the currency as a whole will be discussed in detail later. At this stage suffice it to say that one or two effects may be seen: either the coins of the condemned ruler may vanish into the state melting pot, or, if they are of little intrinsic value, they may be abandoned by their owners and so create an impression of abundance in the currency pool when studied by archaeologists or economists. Either way a false impression will be created unless the political circumstances surrounding the numismatic event are fully appreciated. *Damnatio* does not have to be considered as a phenomenon associated with individuals or only as a phenomenon of antiquity. The coinages of entire regimes may suffer as a result of a change in the political situation; the arrival of Charles II in London and the restoration of the monarchy in 1660, for instance, resulted in the suppression of the coinage of the Commonwealth. This coinage was demonetised on November 30th, 1660 but the edict announcing the intention was issued on September 7th.[5]

It is worth noting that a time-lapse of three months occurred before the new regime suppressed its rival's currency, allowing an interval for the provision of a replacement coinage. Even so, in areas distant from immediate facilities for implementing the withdrawal decision, some Commonwealth coinage will have continued to circulate simply for the convenience of trade for a period beyond this, and estimates suggest a third of the coinage remained unaccounted for even after the last date for its use.

The choice of portrait type may have significance beyond that already outlined, that is the depiction of the ruler in a number of symbolic guises, and it may be used to convey specific information to the user of the coin which either enhances the value of the coin, without increasing its actual intrinsic monetary value, or indicates a change in the structure of the currency in general.

It is reasonable to claim that in most fully developed currency systems where very large numbers of individual coins circulate, the production needs of such a coinage call for the optimum use of technical resources in the reproduction of the dies from which the coinage is produced. Coins should be cheap to manufacture. In the light of this observation let us consider the phenomenon of left-facing portrait coins of the Roman imperial period. Most people are, and always have been, right-handed, and it is normal for a right-handed artist to produce a *left*-facing portrait. So, in cutting a die from which to strike coins the artist will engrave, if there are no other constraints, a left-facing image. On striking such a die an image reversal takes place, producing a *right*-facing impression. Thus the choice of alignment of the portrait is a response to a purely technical problem. When there is deviation from the normal in a coin series we should look to see whether it may represent a significant message conveyed through the medium of the coinage.

From the later first century, after a period of stylistic uncertainty, the Roman mint settled down to the almost invariable practice of producing coins with right-facing busts. In the third century, issues with left-facing busts begin to appear in some profusion and this practice continued into the fourth century and, in the case of some silver coins, right on into the sixth century. What was the reason for this change of style and why do the left-facing coins share the same metalurgical values and reverse types with regular right-facing coins issued at the same time? One feature which distinguishes these coins is that the left-facing emperor is generally shown armed with a spear, shield and helmet, or combination of these adjuncts, or is dressed in elaborate robes and carries a symbol of the consular magistracy, such as a globe or eagle-tipped sceptre (*Plate 5 :4*). A clue to the problem is provided by the coinage of the British usurpers, Carausius and Allectus (286–96).[6] The coins issued by the separatist British regime bear a series of sequence marks which can, in conjunction with other evidence, be arranged into an annual sequence. Within each annual issue are three types with the left-facing bust. As the Roman army was paid three times each year we may feel justified in connecting the issue of the coins with the pay of the army. Since army pay was very low indeed in the third century and had to be supplemented by imperial gifts, which were regularly bestowed as a component of the pay, it may

31

well be that the left-facing coins were issued to pay part, or whole, of this donative. This suggestion is fortified by the occurrence of coins with consular busts, as well as overtly military types, since an imperial consulship was another occasion on which donatives were given to the troops.

We may, thus, trace imperial benefactions by observing when and by whom the left-facing coins were issued. A pattern becomes clear: they were issued to pay donatives on accessions, consulships, as a regular part of military pay and at fixed intervals during the reign when imperial vows for the safety of the state were promulagated. As with any other rule there are exceptions to this scheme since left-facing busts were also used to signal changes in the value of the currency. Two revaluations are exemplified by this signalling. Constantine's reform of 318 produced a spate of left-facing portraits, indicative of a change of value of the coinage without a change in module or metal (*Plate 5 : 5*). Similarly the introduction of a reformed coinage in 348 was accompanied by the use of the left-facing bust on the first denomination of the new series of coins to be issued (*Plate 5 : 6*).

Methods of indicating changing coin values may be less overt than the examples quoted above, especially if the change is in the nature of a disguised devaluation of the currency. In these circumstances a symbol which can be identified by the state, or its officials, may be employed which might be overlooked by the casual user of the coinage in order to facilitate the recovery of the better coin in state transactions, though such practices rarely deceive the citizen for long. An example of this practice may be quoted from the late Byzantine period. When Constantinople was recaptured from the Crusaders in 1268, Michael VIII issued a gold coinage which depicted on the obverse an aerial view of the walls of the city in which stood the Virgin Mary praying over them. The circuit of the wall is shown in clear detail with six groups of triple towers on the perimeter. This design remained unchanged for more than thirty years until the joint reign of Andronikos II and Michael IX (1295–1320), when a debasement took place at about the mid-point of the joint reign and the purity of the gold *hyperperon* fell from *c*.14 carats to *c*.12 carats.[7] At the same time the city walls displayed on the coins changed from an array of six towers to an array of four towers. The change is slight and might even be overlooked, but undoubtedly this device allowed for the easier collection of the higher value coinage by the state from the currency pool without too clearly advertising the change in the value of the coinage to the world at large (*Plate 5 :7, 8*).

We have explored a number of instances in which the obverse of the coin may be used to convey non-monetary information of greater and lesser subtlety and import, but traditionally it is the reverse of the coin which has attracted the attention of students of coinage since this is the area in which the restraints of the need to display a single theme, the ruler, do not operate. We have already suggested that in terms of interpreting programmatic coin types the untrammelled use of the academic imagination may invalidate the evidence which can be legitimately adduced, but there are areas in which information is imparted, either consciously or unconsciously.

If we take a long view of a coinage system, the changing preoccupations witnessed by the choice of reverse types may themselves offer a valuable comment on developments within the society which produced them. We can exemplify this point by a brief consideration of the Roman coinage.

In its earliest issues the concerns of the coinage are exclusively religious in content, but by the second century BC the types, though still alluding to Roman historical or religious themes, have been adapted to the advertisement of the family history of the issuing magistrates, or their patrons. This move towards a personalisation of the coinage accurately reflects the fissiparous nature of the society of the later Republic. The tendency towards using the public coinage as a vehicle of personal advertisement found its culmination in the issues of the war lords who brought about the demise of the Republic. Both Sulla and Caesar set the tone for the use of coin as a propaganda medium in the imperial period. Within this period itself the choice of coin types appears to reflect social or political trends quite well. Apart from the commemoration of individual events, the tone of the coinage may well be taken to reflect individual imperial concerns so that, for instance, the early Julio–Claudian coinage can be seen as reflecting the concern with the establishment of the dynastic idea as a Roman political ideal. The emperor and relatives figure largely, as does the claim to rule by descent from Augustus. Characterising the second century can best be done by an analysis of the types used on the base metal coinage of Antoninus Pius (138–161) and Marcus Aurelius (161–180) in their own names – two reigns which are central to the golden age of the empire. If we count off the types employed into two

33

categories – military and non-military – we find the following:

	Number of reverse types	Percentage of total coin types
Antoninus Pius		
Military types	63	12.3
Non-military	451	87.3
Marcus Aurelius		
Military	87	47
Non-military	98	53

Clearly these proportions reflect something of the preoccupations of the authorities controlling the issue of coins in each reign. The reign of Pius was, in Roman terms, relatively peaceful with warfare frequent but, with the exception of Britain, at a low level. The reign of his adopted successor Marcus was characterised by intensive warfare in the Eastern provinces with the Parthian Empire, and very long and costly campaigns on the Danube which occupied the whole of the second half of the reign.

With the advent of the third century we enter a long period of political turmoil, in which contending military commanders strove for imperial power and the forces of barbarian peoples gathered strength on the frontiers. The tone of the coinage changes to a virtually exclusively military one, or one in which the well-being of the emperor himself holds the pre-eminent position. The frequent use of Pax (peace) as a reverse type exemplifies a fervent hope and not a proclamation of achievement. The emperor's person, in a vain attempt to stave off the nearly inevitable assassination, is coupled with a series of protective deities. Gallienus, murdered in 268, sought the protection of a pantheon of deities – Diana, Neptune, Jupiter and Mercury. His rival, Postumus, murdered in 268 also, invoked the protection of Hercules. Abstract protection proving of no avail, Aurelian (270–75) declared himself to be a god and his coinage is issued with the obverse title inscription reading DEO ET DOMINO NATO AURELIANO AVG (Aurelian the Emperor born god and lord). Aurelian was murdered in 275 and one of his successors, Probus, who also sought lifetime deification, was sent to his heavenly kingdom by disaffected soldiers in 282 after a reign of six years.

These inscriptions and the attribution of protective powers by specific deities to the emperor may be seen as a numismatic reflection of rites, ceremonies and usages which will have been devised to protect the person of the emperor in the real world and for which, in a very badly documented period, we have little or no information. That such protection was sought and that methods to accord it were evolved by removing the imperial person to a remoteness from day to day contact with his subjects can be found in the ceremonials evolved by Diocletian (284–305) and developed fully in the fourth century. This new remoteness is symbolised in the coinage by the use of more abstract portraiture which conventionalised the concept of the remote and serene ruler (*Plate 5 :9*). At the same time, the reverse types reflect both the abstract guardianship role of the emperor rather than his specific feats, of which, in the fourth century, there were remarkably few to be recorded, and the dominance of Christianity as the state religion with a consequent suppression of pagan iconography.

To a great extent this analysis is a subjective one and depends entirely upon our knowledge of events in the Roman world. The coinage confirms what in most cases we already know from other sources. It is not a primary document in its own right, but it does confirm that in the Roman world at least the choice of coin type and portrait style is a reflection of real events and not merely the whim of artist or engraver. The principle may be extended to other coinages where it is likely that a programmatic intention underlies the choice of types. Perhaps most surprising is the suggestion that King Alfred's coinage reflects his successes against the invading Danish army.[8]

CHAPTER THREE

Coinage and the historical record

Because coins often convey explicit allusion to specific events they have been seen as a medium through which history can be written. This view has been held by some numismatists, especially those dealing with the Roman period, and strongly resisted by professional historians. The problem which arises is a simple one. Some coins illustrate known events: a coin issued by Brutus alludes to the assassination of Julius Caesar, the coins of the Visigothic kings of Spain proclaim the capture of individual cities, and the 50-pence piece alludes to Britain joining the European Common Market. These events are all attested by coins and are also all attested by independent documentary evidence so that the deduction made from the observation of the coin is subject to an external check. The coin is simply a gratifying historical extra, an illustration not a revelation. But knowing that coins offer this illustration raises the temptation to try to construct a historical narrative using coins which have no supplementary documentary cross-check. In principle there is nothing wrong with this; documentary sources may not have survived and it would be foolish to reject any sort of information simply because no other account survives. This is fine when the references are specific but where is the line drawn between what is specific and what is inferential? It is on this rock that many a numismatic reputation has been wrecked, with historians rejoicing on the shore.

It is true that the 'pimple and wrinkle' school of numismatic pseudo-historical reconstruction is easy to mock – the emperor's worried look being used as a key to the political history of a reign, or the vacuity expressed in Habsburg portraits measuring the instability of

Central Europe. This is manifest nonsense. It is in the Roman imperial coinage that the greatest reliance has been placed on the interpretation of the historical process through the medium of coins. Roman society used visual imagery as a central feature of its political mechanism; for instance, statues of the emperors were distributed throughout the empire and represented the corporeal imperial presence itself. Public art proclaimed through widely understood imagery the integrity and universality of the Roman state. This art was very sophisticated and, to the perceptive, could be read as clearly as a proclamation. Consider, for example, the great forum constructed by Augustus in the centre of Rome. The axis of this monument was an avenue flanked by statuary which lead the eye to a great figure of Augustus in a triumphal chariot. Each statue in the avenue was of a personality who had physically extended the frontiers of Roman rule. To the knowledgeable spectator there could be no question of the message, with Augustus in a central position at the culmination of an historical process which extended back to Romulus. The critic will say that this may be true but that the average Roman would not rise to this visionary apotheosis by reason of lack of intellect. This is an unascertainable and presumptive claim, but even if it were true the magnificence of the architecture would impress the spectator with the power of the builder so that the *whole* is a comprehensible symbol made up of symbolic parts which can be understood on several cognitive levels. Just so with coins; the coin type may be a récherché and academic image understood by a minority, but the *fact* of the coin, its existence as a product of a political power has a compelling impact on the beholder. When Christ was asked about the payment of taxes to the Roman government of Palestine he drew attention to the imperial image on the coinage: 'Whose image and superscription do you see?' It was, of course, Caesar's image and the questioners were advised to 'Render unto Caesar the things that are Caesar's, and to God the things that are God's'. The image conveyed the message – it was not the figure of Livia on the reverse which made the point but the portrait and titles of Tiberius on the obverse which were important. In another context the image of Livia may have been important in conveying the continuity of familial connection between Tiberius and Augustus through his mother's second marriage.

Coins are primary, contemporary historical documents. They may not tell the truth, the whole truth and nothing but the truth but the wholesale condemnation of coins as a source of historical information is obscurantist. Coins can be used in a number of ways: by observation of direct allusion; by elucidation of indirect allusion, and by field observation of the distribution pattern of coins, either in hoards or as site or single finds.

We have already outlined the sort of direct allusions which can be found on coins: changes of regime, the construction of buildings, the celebration of victories, the conclusion of treaties, and so forth. Some of this information must be looked at with scepticism because it is self-proclamatory – not the objective truth but the 'official' truth. There are any number of instances where the interpretation of coin information can be reinterpreted by the cynical. Gallienus may have proclaimed 'VIBQVE PAX' but his subjects knew that he was at odds with a rival in the west, that his eastern provinces were in the hands of Palmyra and that the Persians were at the gates of Antioch. The claim that 'peace rules everywhere' was true only to the extent that the three contending factions were in a state of mutual exhaustion. Again the wretched state of the late Roman world in which Visigoth and Ostrogoth, Vandal and Burgundian fought over the pickings of the provinces finds no echo in the imperial coinage's constant proclamation of 'The Victories of the Emperors'.

It is to be expected that the best possible construction will always be put on events and that downright lies will sometimes be told. Such lies may not be carefully thought out disinformation, but unconsidered relics which have not been expunged by time. No one would give weight to the claims of the British monarchs to be kings of France, though the claim is published on the coinage until the reign of George III.

Knowing that falsity, archaicism and bland optimism distinguish the content of so many historic coinages, we should perhaps develop a more critical attitude to other numismatic 'information', conveyed in undocumented periods. Some of the kings of Britain who reigned in the century between the invasion of Britain by Julius Caesar and the conquest by Claudius adopted Latin as the medium for their coin inscriptions. This, together with the use of the word 'REX' to indicate their kingly status, has been interpreted as an indication that these rulers enjoyed Roman support, even client status, and that they deployed the implied threat of Roman intervention on their behalf in the political intrigues that mark intertribal relations at this period. There are other interpretations, the simplest of which is that it was thought couth and up-market to grace coinage with Latin legends, or that, by mimesis, the native coins, which were of very variable metallic standards, would participate in the financial integrity of the prestigious Roman currency. Unintelligibility is often a mark of prestige in coinage, and we still defer to the Latin language to the present day in matters monetary.

How do we sort out what to believe and what to treat with scepticism? One approach is to judge the reliability of the information in relation to cases where a check is possible so that we can estimate the overall tendency of the issuer of the coinage under review to be accurate in his output of information.

Let us exemplify this from the coinage of Antoninus Pius (138–61) once again. In the year 154/5 a large number of coins were issued which depict Britannia, the personification of Britain. The type is limited to two denominations, the *dupondius* and the *as*, both low value coins in the middle of the second century (*Plate 6 :1*). There is nothing remarkable about the personification of a province appearing on Roman coins, but such appearances normally indicate some special activity in that province. Types with Britannia had previously been issued by Hadrian and by Pius to commemorate the advances into Caledonia and the erection of the Antonine Wall at the start of the reign. The second issue is unsupported by documentary evidence but distribution studies show that these coins are restricted in circulation to Britain and that they are very common on military sites. It would be logical to associate the coins with a military event; but can this assumption be validated?

The reign of Pius is notoriously badly documented but we know that a number of low intensity wars were fought, though there is a reticence about recording these military events through the medium of the coinage. This was not a bellicose reign. However, the mint of Alexandria produced coins which are conveniently dated on a year-by-year basis, and from time to time this mint produced coins with a figure of Victory (Nike) as the reverse type.[1] Since we can date these issues closely we can try to correlate the coins with the slender documentary evidence for military activity in the reign to see whether they coincide with the military events and commemorate real victories or were issued randomly. Table A shows a level of correlation which is very good and it is clear that a particular clustering takes place in the years between 151 and 154/5. Further, at this period the Rome mint issued the largest number of overtly military types of the entire reign. On this evidence it could be conjectured that a war took place in Britain which lasted for three or four years and which culminated in a donative to the troops paid in the Britannia coins especially produced for the event. A year or two later the army of Britain was reinforced with drafts drawn from Germany and, in the interim, the Antonine Wall was temporarily abandoned and the garrisons withdrawn to Hadrian's Wall – perhaps signalling something less than a total victory.

	Regnal year date	Nike type recorded	Recorded event
2	138–39	x	War in Britain
3	139–40		
4	140–41		
5	141–42	x	Antonine Wall; Pius' 2nd Imperatorial acclamation
6	142–43		
7	143–44	x	} Coins celebrate British
8	144–45	x	victory by Rome mint
9	145–46		
10	146–47	x	?
11	147–48		
12	148–49		
13	149–50	x	Mauretanian campaign
14	150–51		
15	151–52	x	Extension of German frontiers; Coins celebrating 'Spirit of the Army' issued by Rome mint
16	152–53	x	
17	153–54	x	? Rising in Egypt
18	154–55	x	Britannia *Asses* issued
19	155–56		
20	156–57		
21	157–58	x	? Jewish revolt
22	158–59		
23	159–60	x	? War in Dacia
24	160–61	x	Rising in N. Africa

Table A

Here we see how a specific coin type and its distribution leads us into a wider historical perspective. The fourth century provides us with another example of the use of a single coin type to investigate a pattern of events.

In this case the coin is not a specific type in the sense that it records a once and for all event in the manner of the Antonine coin discussed above. Rather the case rests upon the recognition that some coins are issued as an integral part of a specific ceremonial event; just as Maundy coins represent the presentation of charity at a ceremony which may be held in different places, though the nature of the ceremony and the sorts of coins employed remain constant. In the Roman world the peregrinations of the emperor were as widely celebrated as those of today's rulers and special ceremonial and security attended the event. Naturally the paintwork was refreshed, the grass cut and the worst civic eyesores put out of sight and a whole battery of flattery and welcoming gestures employed by the community to be visited. And why not, since an imperial visit would bring benefactions and the remission of unpaid back taxes? By the later third century the ritual was well established. A welcoming committee assembled outside the city, inhabitants lined the route, speeches were made by the emperor and reciprocated by local dignitaries. More significantly for our purposes, a gift of money was distributed to the population. When the visit, technically termed an *Adventus*, was to a city with a branch of the imperial mint, the mint struck special coins in commemoration of the visit to provide the cash for the handout to the populace. Where documents survive there is an exact correlation between the known movements of emperors and the production of these special *Adventvs* coins (*Plate 6:2*) so that it is legitimate to extrapolate from this evidence when the coins appear where there is no supporting documentary record for the event.

In the early fourth century the London mint issued no less than three separate series of *Adventus* coins in the name of Constantine the Great. In the light of the established significance of the coin type we can, with confidence, claim that the London coins indicate that Constantine made three state visits to Britain. One of these visits is mentioned, in an obscure way, by the ecclesiastical historian Eusebius, but his testimony has been overlooked or ignored. The coins validate the text.[2]

Archaeologists, despite protestations to the contrary, set great store by dates. Real firm dates are quite a rarity and there is a natural, but mistaken, tendency to ascribe visible changes in the archaeological record to the specific available dates. So the visit of Constans in 343/4 is a cluster point in text-books and excavation reports and he is credited with initiating changes on Hadrian's Wall, adding to the coastal defences of the south of Britain and tinkering with the administrative structure of the island. Typically all are credited to the known, dated and brief event. Now we have more dates because looking at the coins of Constantine in the light of the rituals of his period we can see that he came to Britain in 307, 312 and 314. We must next ask why and what can we do with this new information? Eusebius tells us that in 312, a date established as a Constantinian visit by the coins, troops were withdrawn from Britain to bolster the forces being assembled to invade Italy, then held by the usurper Maxentius. Such a withdrawal of forces might leave archaeological evidence, specifically in the coin records of garrison forts where we might expect coins to dry up at this moment. There is indeed a group of sites which display in their coin records features which may be ascribed to this event; these are the outpost forts on Hadrian's Wall. Four forts protected the approach to the Wall – High Rochester and Risingham in the east, Netherby and Bewcastle in the west.[3] Traditionally it is considered that these forts were garrisoned until 367, but an examination of the finds from them shows that there is no record of any coin being found which was issued later than 310, a date significantly close to the 312 troop withdrawal and visit date. This is a compelling equation founded upon the identification of a specific event through a study of coin types, distributive studies of coin finds and a documentary source. Each element of the study leads the enquirer to the others.

This fruitful approach to coin studies has brought to light new aspects of the past and brought into question what have been hitherto well-established doctrines. The history of Wales in the late Roman period has been radically revised in the light of coin studies.

Until recently it was an axiom of early Welsh history that Roman forces were evacuated from Wales in 383 by the usurper Magnus Maximus. Further, the legends which placed him in the forefront of the heroes of Welsh history appeared to demonstrate an unbroken historical tradition from the Roman period to the Middle Ages. This tradition was based upon the historical writings of Gildas, whose garbled account of the last years of Roman rule, written in the sixth century, bore apparently irrefutable witness to the part played by Maximus in stripping Britain of its army and leaving it prey to invaders.[4]

This view is flatly refuted by numismatic evidence. Firstly, military sites in Wales, which legend associates with Maximus, produce coins which are later in date than the reign of Maximus; and, since these coins are found in association with military equipment, there is no question of the soldiers having moved out and civilians occupying their place. Detailed examination of the coins shows that the occupation continued to the end of the fourth century and suggests that troops were withdrawn from Wales in a crisis created by the revolt of the usurper Eugenius in 393.[5] Secondly, a detailed study of the gold coinage of Maximus reveals evidence that, far from quitting Britain for good, Maximus returned from his Continental capital, Trier, to London and there struck a type of gold and silver coinage which was of a variety only produced by the mint which travelled around with the court as part of the imperial entourage. Supplementary, literary, evidence suggests that the reason for this return was to fight an important military campaign, probably in the north of Britain (*Plate 6:3*). So despite 1,500 years of literary invention the positive contemporary evidence of the coins awaited their recovery from the soil to set the record straight.[6]

We have seen that the close consideration of coin evidence may shake the foundations of the literary narrative. This is because coins are produced with immediacy in response to events, whereas the literary record is composed after the event, often much after, and can suffer from bias if not outright distortion or suppression of facts. Even when the narrative forms an acceptable body of information it may suffer from imprecision which can be rectified by numismatic evidence.

A neat illustration of this point can be drawn from the Tacitean narrative of events in Britain recorded in the biography of Agricola.[7] Tacitus gives a specific account, though generalised in details, of the career of his father-in-law as governor of Britain. In his six years of command Agricola extended Roman control through the north of Britain and decisively defeated the last native army that could be mustered against Rome at the Battle of Mons Graupius. The battle left Rome in control of the entire island from the south coast to the extremity of Caledonia, a position from which it soon withdrew. The chronology of Agricola's governorship is only obliquely dated by the text of Tacitus. It is known that he served two *triennia*, that is a double gubernatorial term amounting to six years. Tacitus gives a sketchy year-by-year account of the governor's activities, which culminates in the Battle of Mons Graupius and his recall in dubious circumstances by Domitian. The terminal date is established by the fact that the recall followed shortly after Domitian celebrated a triumph for defeating the Chatti in Germany, a victory whose completeness and quality Tacitus regards with great scepticism. Coins of the year 84 proclaim the victory and give Domitian the title Germanicus. All precedents indicate that the assumption of the title and the celebration of the triumph would coincide. Thus Agricola's governorship should have ended in 84 and started six years previously in AD 78, and so the text-books tell it.

Nothing could be clearer except that the practice of the Rome mint was to strike coinage on a cyclical basis. In this system all of the gold coinage was struck, then the silver and so on through the denominations. This cycle seems to have started at the beginning of the year so that, unless a special issue was put out, an event occurring late in a year would not be commemorated on the coinage until the following year when the coining cycle resumed. This seems to have been the case with Domitian's triumph and acclamation. Coins from the mint of Alexandria, with their annual dating inscribed on them, clearly record Domitian as holding the title Germanicus in 83, a full year before it is recorded at Rome.[8]

Egyptian papyri also record this date for the victory. In the light of this the dates of the governorship of Agricola have to be moved back a year to 77–83. This appears to be a trivial matter; after all, some archaeologists date by millennia, and to others a century is but a blink, and a date within a decade an unattainable dream. But the historical implications are quite profound. Let us juxtapose the 'old' scheme of the governorship with the 'new', listing the salient events recorded by Tacitus and adding any known externals such as the demise of Vespasian and Titus (see Table B).

With the new chronology the whole emphasis changes; and instead of the hated Domitian thwarting Agricola's ambitious drive north we now see that it was Titus who called a temporary halt. The year 80 is spent on establishing a frontier and dealing with the Novantae, a tribe which was behind the line already reached by the advance. Only with the accession of Domitian is Agricola allowed to proceed, albeit with reduced forces. It is interesting to note that the inscription found at Verulamium which dates the completion of the forum no longer

'Old' Scheme	'New' Scheme
77	77 Arrives in summer. Campaigns in Wales.
78 Arrives in summer. Campaigns in Wales.	78 Advance to north. Winter spent Romanising province.
79 Vespasian dies (June), Titus succeeds. Advance to north. Inscription at Verulamium mentions Agricola. Winter spent Romanising the province.	79 Vespasian dies, Titus succeeds. Inscription at Verulamium recording Agricola. Campaigns north to Tay.
80 Campaigns north to Tay.	80 Builds fort on Forth Clyde line. Consolidates conquests.
81 Builds fort on Forth/Clyde line. Consolidates conquests. Titus dies (September), Domitian succeeds.	81 Novantae conquered. Titus dies, Domitian succeeds.
82 Novantae conquered.	82 Troops withdrawn for German war. Advance north of Forth/Clyde.
83 Troops withdrawn for German war. Advance north of Forth/Clyde.	83 Further advance north. Battle of Mons Graupius. Recall.
84 Further advance north. Battle of Mons Graupius. Recall.	84

Table B

coincides with the second winter of Agricola's governorship, a period in which he was engaged in a vigorous campaign of encouragement of building and adoption of Roman manners of life among the native population. The structure will in any event have been started long before Agricola arrived in Britain.

We have seen that lies, distortions and misunderstandings can be contradicted by the contemporary numismatic evidence when the coins themselves are of a special type. We can look at the problems from another point of view, where it is not a specific coin but the distribution of coins which points to a contradiction of historical sources.

The Byzantine historian Procopius composed a number of historical works which give very detailed accounts of the reign of the emperor Justinian (527–565). One of these works was a 'Secret History' which contradicted the accounts in his other published works and which put the worst possible complexion on the actions of the emperor, his wife and his court; nothing is too bad for Procopius.[9] One of his most explicit claims is that Justinian stopped the pay of the troops guarding the frontiers of the empire and that, in consequence, the soldiers deserted their posts leaving the borders forever unguarded and open to the enemy. Such an event might be expected to show up in the coin records for the frontier forts and adjacent sites with a dramatic drop in coinage reaching them. But a detailed survey of all the coinage of the reign of Justinian found in frontier forts or in the immediate vicinity shows no such thing.[10] Forts on the Danube, hoards found along the Euphrates, towns on the Persian frontier all show an undiminished flow of coins before, during and after the period during which the pay was supposed to have been stopped and the forts deserted. Only in one small corner of the empire does the flow stop and that is in southern Palestine. Since Procopius himself came from this area we may conjecture that he exaggerated a local incident into an empire-wide scandal. His words have carried weight with historians but the coins give the lie to his narrative.

These illustrations are of interest at the micro-historical level; they are pieces of research which reinforce or slightly correct extant accounts of events, and the research techniques work quite well because we have half of the equation to start with. Problems arise when the non-numismatic check is removed and the coins themselves are used both to pose the questions and to supply the answers.

There are coin-issuing societies with little or no historical narrative to give life to their artefacts. Can coins help the archaeologist and historian to achieve an insight into the behaviour of these peoples? Let us turn our attention to the coinage of the tribes of Britain and Gaul in the last three centuries BC. Here we have a prolific coinage issued by discrete political communities who have only the shadowiest existence in ancient written sources.[11]

Coinage found among the Celtic peoples of Gaul falls into three broad categories. Firstly there are genuine Greek coins which have been imported from the Mediterranean world or from among the Greek settlers who founded colonies on the fringes of the Celtic world, as at Marseilles, Antibes, Nice or Ampurias. The second category consists of copies of Greek coins, normally of gold issues; and the third category is represented by the introduction of a fractional currency of silver or bronze coins into what had, hitherto, been a high-value, largely gold unit, system.

The three broad categories represent temporal shifts. As far as we can judge, the earliest phase of coin use was restricted to Greek coins, the next development was of the high value copies and the last the introduction of fractional coins.

We can note these changes and record the fact of the existence of the coins but we can also try to develop an explanation of what happened in the past to produce the observed effect. When archaeologists are short of direct information they approach the past by postulating hypotheses or theories which seem to account for the data which is available. The jargon for this is 'modelling' and a hunch, guess or shot in the dark is called a model. Can a model be constructed to account for the behaviour of Celtic coinage in its development? Let us examine the coinage in the west, especially Gaul, where the narratives of Caesar and other classical authors throw some light on events at the very end of the period under consideration.[12]

Our classical authors tell us that Celtic mercenary soldiers were very much in demand for service in the armies of the Greek kingdoms in the third and second centuries BC, so that it seems reasonable to equate the occurrence of Greek coins with this factor. We know that cash payments were made to the leaders of Greek war bands and that these payments were distributed to the rank and file by the leaders. Much of this coinage will have been used to purchase luxuries that were not available in the Celtic homeland so that the coins will have been recycled straight back into the economy of the Greek world. Other coins will have been used as a source of metal from which to manufacture the intricate jewellery which has been found on Celtic sites. A little will have been retained in its original form to be taken home by the mercenaries and it is this tiny residue in the Celtic homeland with which we are dealing.

Once coinage had been established as the fitting and acceptable medium for the hiring of mercenaries we may hypothesise that the accumulation of wealth in the hands of individuals might have led to social tensions and that the wealthy themselves might have needed to hire mercenaries to fight in not Greek but Celtic wars: wars conducted to establish the dominance of individuals as tribal leaders or of groups of tribes. Since Greek coinage was established by usage as the medium through which mercenaries were paid, it behoved the aspiring employer to produce something as near to the acceptable military currency as he could contrive; and, since this was gold coin of Philip II of Macedon, a coinage used and struck long after his death, it was this which, in various degrees of deviation from the canons of Hellenistic arts, they produced (*Plate 6 :4, 5*).

The third stage of the currency, in this model, arises directly from the second. We would suppose that political stability had been achieved out of struggle, that with this stability came the establishment and recognition of separate tribal states and that these states comprised individual communities. These were not quite towns as the classical world would recognise them, but large settlements with many of the functions of towns and few, if any, of the classical amenities. Such stable quasi-states would tend to individualise their currency, which is no longer geared to mercenary payments, and distinctive types would appear. Further, fractional coins would be needed in commerce in the proto-urban centres and to pay officials, magistrates and employees of the community who, like the Greek jurymen cited earlier, could not produce their own subsistence and would have to purchase it for cash from those who could. Thus far we have a model which is built upon observed and ascertainable changes in the coinage over a period of time. Is it true? There is no way of knowing, and alternative models can be built on the same body of data. For instance, we could look at the last part of the hypothesis, which sees fractional coins as an element implying stability of administration and state formation where there had hitherto been only successful or unsuccessful individuals holding power by force of arms, in quite another light.

The development of petty currency in late medieval Britain can be used as a model to reinterpret the development of the same sort of currency in the prehistoric Celtic world. Small change in England grew because of mobility, itself an expression of a profound change in the structure of society. When communities were no longer cohesive units, the need for the immediate payment of obligations became imperative. Credit is not granted to the passing stranger, so a token coinage evolved with which to settle small transactions. Lead tokens were produced and sold in multiples for real high value coin to users of ferry services across the Thames. Monastic houses and parishes issued tokens to their parishioners on organised pilgrimages which could be used in other monastic houses or in inns on the pilgrimage route. These would be accumulated and redeemed by the issuing ecclesiastical authority after the pilgrimage season. So trivial coin is equated with movement, itself a broadening of the life style of individuals but also with a growth of commercial distrust. Just such a model may pertain in Celtic society – the arrival of fractional base metal coins showing a loosening of social units, not a tightening. It may be significant that one of the most prolific fractional coinages is that of Cunobelin, possibly a king of the Catuvellauni or, more likely, the Trinovantes, whose kingdom may have spread over most of south-east Britain in the decades before the Claudian invasion, and that most of the extant specimens have turned up on religious sites – themselves, no doubt, places of pilgrimage.[13]

We can extend our hypothetical reinterpretation back to the second phase of Celtic coinage: the high value copies of Greek originals. Part of the reason for interpreting these as payments to domestic mercenaries lies in their apparent unsuitability for use as a currency for small transactions, although it does not follow that a currency of large denominations prevents petty transactions taking place through its medium. In short, it is not necessarily a heroic coinage reserved for use in a restricted range of transactions which are exclusively the concern of warriors and the aristocracy, such as ransom, bride purchase or the maintenance of followers. Such a coinage system can work perfectly well in a society which has small, immobilised community units and a developed credit system. Again, medieval parallels offer an insight on which to base our model. Merchants and suppliers of goods and services covered a wide range of territory and had dealings with a large number of communities. Credit was given for purchases and the debt 'put on the slate' until the total individual debt reached the level at which it could be discharged within the prevailing currency system. As we have noted, this operation requires a social system in which obligations are recognised and can, in some way, be enforced. It is one in which the debtor cannot do a flit on the approach of the creditor – it is not a mobile society. Using this model we could see the middle period of Celtic coinage as representing just such a stable, well-ordered stage of socio-political evolution rather than one of strife and turmoil. Radically different models can, thus, be formulated from a set of numismatic data when there is little external evidence against which to judge its original significance. But this demonstration of alternative models should not be used to condemn the use of such reconstructive processes because out of such struggle comes enlightenment.

CHAPTER FOUR

Coin hoards

Coin hoards are inextricably mixed up with the idea of buried treasure and everyone gets excited about that subject. The law itself has special regulations to investigate hoards which have remained unchanged since early medieval times, and public interest is roused by press accounts of spectacular finds of coins. Then there are those films in which the hero fights his way through horrific hazards to find the loot. It is the realisation of all our dreams when, in the last scene, he reaches the treasure cave and trickles the shiney stuff through his fingers: lahks of rupees, myriad moidres, écus, pieces of eight, sequins and golden guineas. And there's something for his nubile girlfriend, who tries on the tiaras and necklaces for size. Treasure Island and Aladdin's cave exert a powerful influence, but the whole romantic ambience in which hoards exist serves only to obscure their archaeological reality.

First we should establish just what constitutes a hoard. For practical purposes the minimum size for a hoard is just two coins and the qualifying factor which creates a hoard is that the coins should have been brought together in a deliberate manner. This excludes from consideration associations of coins which have accumulated in archaeological strata over a period of time by normal factors of loss or chance. Of course, most hoards consist of more than two coins, but size alone is not an important qualification for a collection of coins to comprise a hoard. Hoarding seems to be endemic and can be associated with every economic strata of society and with every sort of coin-using community. Within this wide spectrum, coin hoards consisting of what might properly be called treasures coexist with trivial sums of low denomination coins. But the value of these hoards to their original owners may, of course, have been in inverse proportion to their apparent intrinsic value: the loss of a fortune to a rich man may be nothing compared to the loss of the price of the next meal to a starving one. Similarly, the value of a hoard when concealed should not be confused with its modern commercial value; coins which may have been of trivial value in their own day may now have an inflated value by reason of their rarity, or the excellence of the condition of their preservation, or any other factor which has nothing at all to do with their place on the monetary system of which they formed an original element.

There are, however, hoards of such spectacular nature that they cannot but excite curiosity about the motives for their concealment, the reason for their non-recovery and the sheer physical problems which must have been experienced by those who hid them in the first place. How were the 80,000 gold coins of the late Republic, which were found at Modena in Italy in the eighteenth century, actually hidden? How many people were involved? How were they persuaded to keep the secret? How many sleepless nights did they experience wondering if the treasure was safe or whether a colleague in the know was already out for a bit of surreptitious midnight shovelling? And, finally, why was the hoard not recovered by those who concealed it?[1]

Most coin hoards which come to the attention of archaeologists are from the ancient world. The reason for this is simply that the period from the invention of coinage until the demise of the western Roman currency system is the one in which the largest numbers of coin-using people existed in an economy which offered a multiplicity of denominations for all levels of coin accumulation to take place and without the mechanism of banks and savings schemes for surplus wealth to be invested. But this fact should not disguise the fact that hoards cover all times and all societies. The earliest hoard, that from the foundations of the temple of Diana at Ephesus, is as old as the invention of coinage itself and the latest is being accumulated at this very moment. Every sort of coin or monetary unit has come to light, from Iron Age currency bars to bundles of five pound notes. Further, nearly everyone has formed a hoard at some time or other. It may be known as the 'extravagance fund', the 'holiday kitty', the 'funny money' or it may be the coins put aside to ease the payment of the telephone account. These sums may be accumulated in piggy banks, old whisky bottles, cocoa tins and concealed under the bed, in the garden shed or be on plain view on the kitchen shelf.

These are temporary immobilisations of coin put together with the intention of returning them to the currency pool sooner or later. The object of the exercise is not primarily to accumulate a coin hoard but to create future spending power. In the light of this we could claim that the hoards which archaeologists and numismatists study represent failure because, with few exceptions such as votive deposits, the intention of the hoarder must always have been to recover the money and to spend it, not to let it lie in the ground, fester in the rafters or rot in the cocoa tin. We should regard the occurrence of a hoard as an exceptional event and ask, not 'why is this hoard here?' but 'why was this hoard not recovered?' The answer to the question may be a simple one: the owner died and the knowledge of the location of the hoard died with him. In every generation a proportion of the unrecovered hoards may be attributable to this cause, but when lots of hoards occur, clustering around a single date, then we must ask what general event could have created a pattern of non-recovery. As we shall see, there is no single cause of non-recovery, least of all can military events be equated with hoarding in a simplistic manner.

A good point from which to initiate any discussion of coin hoards is from the best documented of all, that buried by Samuel Pepys in 1667.[2] In early June, 1667, the Dutch fleet penetrated the defences of the Medway and destroyed the English fleet at anchor. Fearing an immediate attack on London, Pepys gathered up the money which he had on hand and sent it, in the care of his wife and father, to his country house at Brampton in Huntingdonshire. All sorts of disasters struck this enterprise. En route to Brampton the money bags, containing £1,300 in gold, flew out of the coach and split open on the public highway. On reaching their destination, Pepys' wife and father, now burdened with a further £3,000 sent by messenger from London, had to learn the art of hoarding the hard way. Neither was equipped by nature or temperament for hard physical labour nor were they equipped with any large measure of common sense, though their unique situation may have contributed to their subsequent actions. In broad daylight they buried the gold in the front garden of the house (though on a Sunday when the neighbours were at church), and promptly forgot the exact place of concealment.

It was nearly four months later that Pepys judged the political situation to be stable enough for the money to be recovered. Furious to find that his wealth was in the front garden, and terrified of the reaction of the neighbours if they saw him hauling bags of gold out of the flower beds, Pepys chose a dark night to recover his fortune. Alas, not only had father forgotten where it was hidden but he was also stone deaf, thus adding to Pepys' troubles because he could not shout at father to indicate the location of the money but only hiss at him, for fear of rousing the neighbours. A good deal of lantern-lit digging took place before the idea of probing for the bags with an iron spit was conceived. Using this device the bags were found, but the employment of poor excavation techniques spread the coins throughout the soil and over a wide area, the problem being compounded by the fact that the bags had rotted during their interment. Eventually, after sieving and washing lumps of soil in a bucket of water, all but £20 of the original sum was recovered.

Pepys' misadventures give an insight into a number of aspects of hoarding. First, the hoard falls into a category which may be classified as an 'emergency hoard'. This type of hoard, which is deposited on impulse, is one in which the coins have not been especially selected but are just what is on hand when the crisis arises that creates the impulse to hide the coins. Then we should note that the hoard was concealed in a place which was two removes from the event that led Pepys to hide his wealth. The Dutch were on the Medway at Chatham; Pepys was in London, about sixty miles away, and the coins were concealed at Brampton about eighty miles north of London. A sub-hoard may have been created en route to Brampton when the money bags leaped out of the coach and split in the roadway, or the missing £20 may have been overlooked in the frantic nocturnal dig in the garden and may be there to this day. In any event, the recovery of £20 would provide evidence of only an unrepresentative fraction of the original hoard and this might be found in a completely fortuitous location.

Let us imagine that Pepys did not recover his hoard and that a later generation brought it to light. What are the conclusions that could be drawn from its discovery? If we took the coins as the only evidence, we might conclude that the owner of the house at Brampton kept very large sums of money on the premises and we might speculate on how he made his money and what was his local standing. We would look to see whether this degree of wealth was evidenced elsewhere in the vicinity and, if it were not, construct a hierarchy of sites in which the Brampton property occupied a pre-eminent position. We would speculate as to what local problem had caused the burial of the coins

54

and perhaps, because the coins were concealed in the front garden in a spot open to public view, suggest that the rest of the population had fled leaving the panic stricken owner of the coins privacy to hide his wealth in a public place. None of these conclusions is correct. The weath was not created in Brampton – it was made by taking bribes in London for the awarding of naval contracts. There was no trouble in Huntingdonshire and the news of the success of the Dutch fleet probably only reached the area with the arrival of the hysterical Mrs Pepys; and, finally, the location of the hoard in the garden signifies nothing more than the foolishness of those charged with its concealment. Nevertheless, none of the conclusions drawn or questions posed in the hypothetical case outlined above is intrinsically unreasonable if deductions are drawn from the coins and their location alone. When drawing such conclusions from hoard evidence the factors operating in the case of Pepys' hoard must always be borne in mind.

Hoards, as we have noted, fall into various categories, and these categories have been extended and contracted by various schools of numismatic and archaeological researchers into various degrees of elaboration. Here we will consider three classes of hoards.

In discussing Pepys' hoard we noted that it could be characterised as an emergency hoard since it was deposited on an impulse and would have consisted of the coins which were on hand when the emergency arose. In this regard an emergency hoard can be contrasted with a savings hoard, which may have been accumulated over a period of time and added to at intervals. In this event the coins may be actually stratified in their container in a dated sequence. Excavation of the hoard from its container is therefore essential and careful note must be taken of the relative position of each coin as it is removed. Never, never tip the coins out in the first flurry of discovery. Of course, such a hoard must be accessible to the saver so that additions and withdrawals can be made from time to time, and we would expect that hoards found on domestic sites would very largely fall into this category. Savings hoards can display curious features which reflect the inclination of the owner and the sort of coins he could afford to save. For instance, such a hoard might consist of only a single denomination and comprise only the best specimens available to the hoarder. Sometimes such a hoard may consist of coins which fit a special container – a pot which will only allow small silver coins through its mouth cannot be used to hoard large coppers.

When hoards from the ancient world are classified it is sometimes difficult to establish whether the hoard under review is an emergency hoard or a savings hoard, especially if gold coins are concerned. Using the observation that there is a predeliction, if they have the time, for savers to accumulate the best coins, it has been established that the distinction can be made on metrological grounds. Ancient coins were struck with significant variations in the weight of individual specimens around the theoretical or desired weight norm for any series. Ideally a *solidus*, the standard gold coin of the late Roman period, should have weighed c.4.55 grammes, but some were slightly heavier and some slightly lighter. By weighing the individual coins in hoards it has been found that hoarders favoured the collection of a high proportion of heavier coins. Obviously this choice could not be made in crisis conditions, and hoards showing this feature can be classified as savings hoards. Of course there is nothing to prevent a savings hoard being snatched from its domestic deposit place in a crisis and used to form an emergency hoard in some other location, but it would nearly be impossible to make this distinction in normal circumstances and the mere possibility of such an event emphasises the extreme difficulty and ambiguity of interpretation of hoard evidence.

A further characteristic of the emergency hoard is the randomness of the sum comprising the hoard and the frequent inclusion of precious metal objects and jewellery. It would be naïve to believe that all emergency hoards were deposited by the legitimate owners of the contents; it is perfectly possible that such hoards also encompass stolen goods concealed until a hue and cry had died down, as well as plunder hidden by looters. Some emergency hoards are quite spectacular in their composition, especially in the non-numismatic items. The Beaurains hoard, discovered just outside Arras in northern France, contained not only regular gold coins and medallions but silver candlesticks, rings and medallic gold coins set in elaborate gold mounts.[3] The hoard was buried in the early fourth century but a large part of the gold coins in the hoard consisted of issues which had been obsolete as currency for a century before the burial of the hoard and which must have been preserved as a treasure of bullion for decades.

Occasionally a hoard is met with which represents an exact sum of money. Such hoards are likely to represent savings accumulated in order to make a specific payment of a fixed sum – like saving to pay for the television licence. A hoard of this type is the Gornoslav hoard, found in central Bulgaria in 1961, which consisted of 786 gold coins buried shortly after 1185. In 1189 Frederich Barbarossa crossed the area during the preparation for the Third Crusade. In doing so he plundered the Balkans, and the Gornoslav hoard has convincingly been shown to have been hidden to avoid loss to the Crusaders. The sum comprises exactly the amount needed to pay the annual salaries of the monks of the Monastery of Bachkova (for which accounts exist), on whose land it was found in the site of a chapel some miles from the monastery.[4]

Our third category of hoard is the 'purse hoard'. At its simplest such a hoard should be very easy to identify. The contents, even if the container has perished, are usually found in a compact mass which sometimes retains the shape of the purse, and comprise a small number of coins since, on the whole, no one carries heavy sums for their day-to-day business. The coins will normally be a random sum made up of a variety of denominations representing a cross section of the day-to-day currency of the period of their loss. Such hoards are of great interest to the archaeologist because they are the result of a random event, the accidental loss of coins which have not suffered selection by the loser. They should show which coins were in contemporary use and for how long individual issues continued in circulation, so giving an index of the reliability for dating of individual coins found in archaeological strata. A small hoard of this kind was found during the excavations of the Roman fort at Piercebridge in County Durham. During the first remetalling of Dere Street, the road to the north, an unlucky worker dropped his purse which was immediately buried under a mass of gravel. The contents of the purse came to light cemented together in a small bag-shaped mass. This mass resolved itself into a collection of eight *denarii* and two *sestertii*. The silver coins consisted of issues of Vespasian in very worn condition; others of Trajan, also very worn; Hadrian, which was less abraded, and unworn coins of Marcus Aurelius, Faustina I and Lucilla. The date of the loss of the coins can be approximately established by the date of issue of the latest coin. This was an issue in the name of Lucilla, the daughter of Marcus Aurelius, which dates to 164–9. The latest coin in use in the daily transactions of the person who lost the coins was nearly 100 years older than the earliest coin. This sort of evidence can be replicated from finds of other periods and confirms the longevity of coins in circulation which other strands of evidence also establish.

Having characterised hoards, what conclusions may legitimately be drawn from them? We can divide the enquiry into two parts: the numismatic and the historical. The former encompasses the information about coins themselves which can be derived from hoard studies, and the latter the inferential evidence which temporal and distributional studies can yield.

It is the study of hoards which has permitted the numismatist to bring order to the sequence of issues of coin series which are not in themselves intrinsically datable. Let us take the hypothetical case of a coinage which emanates from a state with no recorded history. Such a state is not entirely imaginary; there are a number of coin-issuing peoples for whom history has left no recorded annals or, at best, only the most exiguous records, and there are periods even in otherwise well-recorded societies in which the coins are the only continuous source of historical information. However, let us return to our extreme case and assume that the minimum sort of information which would be sought at the outset of a historical investigation of this society would be to establish a relative framework of the political structure of the state. In short, an attempt would be made to establish the order of the rulers of the state, the relative lengths of their reigns, and the possible economic policies which might be reflected in the sort of coinage they issued. An approach to the solution of these problems could be made through the study of hoards. Let us build on our assumptions and postulate that our anonymous society has yielded a large number of hoards of its coins.

Within a hoard we may confidently expect that there will be coins which show varying signs of wear and that the degree of wear will be related to the circulation life of the coins before they were immobilised in the hoard. As a broad rule the older the coin the greater the wear, so that the oldest coin in a hoard will normally show more wear than the newest or latest. In a series of overlapping hoards we would expect to find coins of the same issue in various states of wear: in an unworn condition when they occupy a position contemporary with a hoard's date of deposit, and worn when they are incorporated in a hoard deposited long after their date of entry into the currency pool. We have, as an example, two hoards. If in one Issue X is found unworn and in the second it is very worn, we can say that the second hoard postdates the other hoard. We can also say that coins more worn than Issue X in Hoard I are earlier than Issue X and that coins found in less

worn conditions in Hoard II are later than Issue X. We thus have a link
between two hoards which puts them into a relative sequence. Should
the terminal coins of the second hoard overlap in the same manner
with yet another hoard, we would have a further link in a chain of
numismatic evidence which is establishing a relative chronology of
coins and, with it, a sequence of the rulers manifested on the coins.
Inevitably the real numismatic world is by no means as straightforward as our hypothetical model, but no matter how difficult the
problems to be overcome the principles governing the establishment
of relative coin sequences remain the same. Within such a sequence we
may observe that some rulers are more frequently represented than
others, or that they show signs of ageing on their coin portraits and/or
that issues in the established relative sequence exhibit differences of
alloy or fineness, allowing the scholar of the series to conjecture on the
relative regnal lengths of the rulers represented and changes in their
financial fortunes.

We have exemplified principles from an extreme case in a postulated
single currency. In reality, hoards often contain coins from more than
one source of issue and absolute dates can be attached to otherwise
undated issues by their association in hoards with attributed issues
from well-dated series. The classic case of such associative dating is
that of the establishment of the inception date of the Roman *denarius*.[5]
Argument has raged since the time of Pliny about the date at which
Rome introduced the silver coin which her armies took to the corners
of her empire. The matter has been settled by the occurrence of
unworn specimens of the earliest *denarii* in a hoard on a site destroyed
in 211 BC and in association with datable coins of a Greek ruler of Sicily
who reigned between 215 and 214 BC. The association of *denarii* with
coins of Hieronymus of Sicily, even without the evidence from Livy
for the date of the destruction of Morgantina, would have given a date
for the introduction substantially different from that recorded by Pliny
or other dates evolved by numismatics from typological studies.

Hoards may also prove to be the best sources of information on the
frequency of coins within the issues of individual rulers or states.
Heavy reliance has been placed in this work on the evidence which can
be deduced from the Antonine coinage in the Reka Devnia hoard, and
similar frequency graphs have been produced in relation to the volume
of English coinage produced by individual moneyers in the medieval
period. The most complete reliance on hoard evidence as an index of

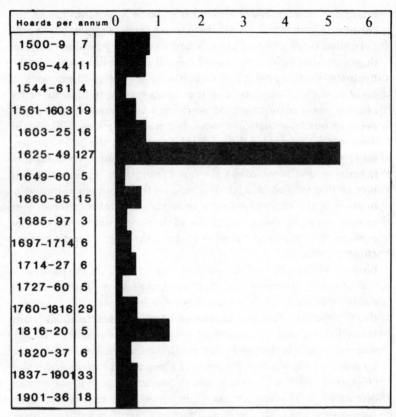

Hoards per annum		0	1	2	3	4	5	6
1500–9	7							
1509–44	11							
1544–61	4							
1561–1603	19							
1603–25	16							
1625–49	127							
1649–60	5							
1660–85	15							
1685–97	3							
1697–1714	6							
1714–27	6							
1727–60	5							
1760–1816	29							
1816–20	5							
1820–37	6							
1837–1901	33							
1901–36	18							

3. Hoards in Britain – medieval to modern period (after Brown and Dolley, 1971).

coin production is that undertaken by M.H. Crawford in the field of Roman Republic coin studies. The implications of this study in the economic field will be examined elsewhere (*Chapter 4*); here we may observe that hoards preserve the relative frequency of coins in the monetary pool in better detail than site finds. This is simply because hoards are often formed to preserve, as an investment, coins which, because of their composition, are under threat of recall and remelting. Coins thus hoarded are withdrawn from the very circulation pool from which site finds derive to the detriment of their representation as casual losses.

Having considered some of the human and numismatic aspects of hoard studies, let us now turn to consider locational aspects of the subject.

In discussing the circumstances surrounding Pepys' hoard we saw that an uncritical spatial analysis of hoard evidence, albeit using a hypothetical model, could mislead. Simple explanations of human behaviour are not always the best explanations and we need to be cautious when attributing motives to the deposition of archaeological evidence. None the less, the hoarding of coins may reasonably be associated with anxiety to protect and preserve wealth. As we have said, hoarding is a constant process but there are moments at which hoarding appears to accelerate. We use the word 'appears' advisedly because an exponential rise in the number of hoards may not be because more are buried but because fewer are recovered. If the number of hoards originally committed to hiding places is roughly constant, then the effect of non-recovery will be to produce the same effect as intermittent increases in hoarding. Certainly, hoards seem to be associated with times of crisis.

A study of coin hoards in Britain from the early medieval period to modern times (*Figure 3*) shows a clear peak of deposits in the years of the Civil War.[6] A superficial view of this cluster of hoards might interpret their spatial distribution as indicating the areas in which the war was fought and in which the population was most directly affected by military events in the years 1641 to 1649. If we plot the hoards (*Figure 4*) in relation to the major battles and sieges there is a striking discrepancy between conflicts and coin hoards.[7] Only the siege of Newark seems to have produced a hoard cluster. On the other hand, the areas in which hoards occur do correspond very closely to those from which it is known that the rival factions recruited their armies. It appears that soldiers concealed their money at home when they left for the campaigns, and these unrecovered hoards probably represent the property of casualities in the conflict. A similar pattern can be discerned in hoards which cluster very markedly at times of political crisis – for example, the Roman Republic, where hoards show the recruiting grounds of Sulla and Marius, or Caesar and Pompey, and not the areas in which their internicene wars were fought (*Figure 5*).[8] A closer look at hoards from the modern period reinforces this point. Analysing the hoards from England we find that there are twenty-one for the period covered by the Napoleonic wars.[9] The distribution throughout the country of these hoards is shown in Table C.

Northumberland	1	Berkshire	1
Cumberland	1	Oxfordshire	2
Yorkshire	3	London	3
Lincolnshire	2	Essex	1
Staffordshire	1	Kent	1
Warwickshire	1	Sussex	1
Worcestershire	1	Hampshire	5
Nottinghamshire	1	Devonshire	1
Gloucestershire	2		

Table C

The coverage is nationwide and partly reflects centres of population and wealth such as York, London and Lincoln. But areas which might be expected to bear the brunt of a French invasion, and this was constantly expected, such as Kent, Essex and Sussex do not produce large numbers of hoards, though these may have been created and recovered when the crisis passed. On the other hand, a quarter of all hoards are found in Hampshire. Can an explanation be offered for this? Possibly so, because there seems to be a compelling equation between the stationing of the fleet at Portsmouth and the recruitment of its crews through the use of press gang, and the large number of hoards found in this region.

In archaeological literature the association of hoarding with impending disaster appears to be irresistable, and the evidence which has been brought forward to this point in the discussion seems to support this view to the extent that the bulk of unrecovered hoards, which is not necessarily the same thing as the number originally concealed, cluster at times of political or military upheaval. But there are circumstances in which hoards remain unrecovered, not because a personal disaster overtook the owner but because an economic disaster overtook the coins which made up the hoards. Sorting out which interpretation to place on hoard evidence is, however, not always easy.

A case in point is the spread of coin hoards in Gaul and Britain in the second half of the third century. There is ample evidence which is witness to the devastation brought about by the invasion of Gaul by Germanic tribes from beyond the Rhine in this period. Raids are known to have occurred in 254, 259 and between the years 268 and 278. Most of the destruction was, ironically, wrought by Roman hands as imperial and urban authorities dismantled public buildings to gain

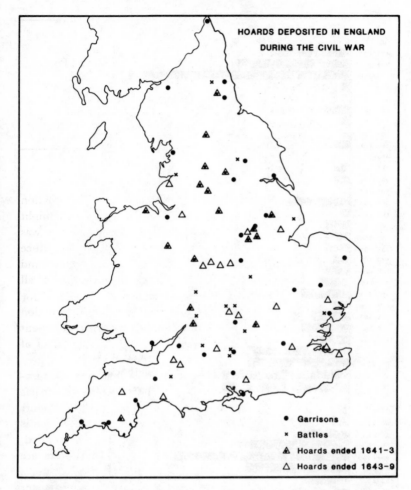

4. Hoards, battles and garrisons of the Civil War (after Kent, 1974, with additions).

materials for hastily erected defences for the unwalled cities. In the countryside rural sites as far south as the foothills of the Pyrenees show signs of destruction in this period. Let us look at the coin hoards which are normally seen as evidence for the advance of raiders into Gaul. We will concentrate on the later period of raids.

The hoards in question consist of coins of the later years of the Gallic

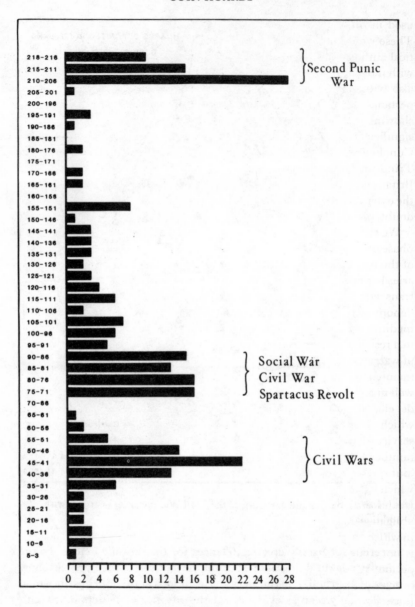

5. Roman Republican coin hoards (after Crawford, 1969).

Empire – the separatist regime which ruled Gaul, Britain and Germany between 258 and 273. Effectively, the issues hoarded are those of Victorinus (268–70) and Tetricus (270–73) together with copies of the regular coinage. These coins represent the nadir of the Roman imperial currency system as established by Augustus and modified by Caracalla. The hoards are made up of double-*denarii*, weighing on average 2.6 grammes and containing about three per cent of silver (effectively 0.78 grammes of silver per coin). With the fall of the Gallic Empire and the re-establishment of central control of the western provinces, Aurelian attempted a reform of the coinage which sought to demonetise the Gallic issues but which probably only succeeded in further reducing their value, since they continued to circulate in the absence of large-scale supplies being maintained of the improved, reformed currency. To supplement the shortfall local copies of Gallic coins were produced and numismatic evidence shows that this copying continued into the reign of Probus (276–82).

Thus far we can trace the chronology of the currency, but the coins are not necessarily evidence of barbarian raids in Gaul. It appears that Probus' policy was to suppress both the base Gallic coinage and their copies. Naturally the pursuit of this policy will have created a horizon of abandoned hoards. The intrinsic value of the coins is negligible, their remelted value less than the cost of rendering them down into their component elements of bronze and a vestigial quantity of silver.

How do we choose between conflicting hypotheses? We have the apparently attractive notion that these hoards represent an unease or even invasion, but the monetary evidence points clearly towards abandonment for purely economic reasons. The hoards are simply the sort of hoards which were accumulated at all periods but fossilised by an exceptional monetary event. The fact that they concur, roughly, with political disturbance is coincidental.

This conclusion is reinforced by the evidence from Britain. Exactly the same sort of hoards are found as those in war-ravaged Gaul in a pattern which covers the whole of the island under Roman control. But Britain was not war-ravaged, its towns were not hastily defended; its garrisons were, if anything, run down. Archaeologists have argued that the hoards indicate that a threat of disaster was felt.[10] Of course, this is a circular argument summed up in the phrase 'threats mean hoards, hoards mean threats'. If it is to be argued that the Gallic hoards were not recovered because of the death or capture of their owners at the hands of barbarians, how are we to explain the non-recovery in Britain which, even if threatened, still has the property of its undisturbed inhabitants in the soil after the crisis had passed? Clearly attempts to use the distribution pattern of hoards in Gaul to establish the routes of barbarian invasions are misguided if the coin hoards are the product of financial rather than military problems.

We have, hitherto, concentrated on relatively negative aspects of hoard studies, pointing out the problems of excessively optimistic or simplistic interpretations of evidence. What are the positive aspects?

At the lowest level we have the preservation of coins which, owing to the attrition suffered by currencies under the impact of economic change, do not survive as site finds and which permit a more complete reconstruction of a currency system than would otherwise be possible. We can also use hoard evidence as an index of the degree to which coin users perceived, or anticipated, changes in the structure of the monetary system. Successive debasements of precious metal coins are normally accompanied by hoards which discriminate in favour of premium coins, often those immediately antecedent to the debasement or coins from an earlier generation which have not yet been forced out of circulation by fiscal pressure. A typical hoard responding to such pressures is that from Dorchester, Dorset, consisting of third-century coins in which the hoarder, faced by the very abrupt decline in the intrinsic value of the silver coinage which took place between 258 and 268, assembled as many high silver content coins as could be obtained[11] (*see Table D*).

We can see that the owner of the Dorchester hoard discriminated in favour of the coinage of Gordian III and Philip and tried to avoid those coins, which must have been relatively easy to obtain, of the period around the closure date of the hoard. It is worth noting that the next issue, not included in the hoard at all, fell to a silver content of only 0.4 grammes.

A last point before we leave hoards is that an important consideration in the interpretation of hoard evidence is the means by which hoards are recovered. Until the advent of the electronic metal detector, the overwhelming majority of hoards were discovered in the course of agricultural work. The plough, not the archaeologist's trowel, has been the most important agent of disinterring hoards. It follows from this that recorded hoards are nearly all located in zones of arable agriculture and that hoards are very rarely recorded from areas in

	Dorchester hoard (Burial date c.260)			
Issuer	Date	Coins in hoard	Coins/Years of issue	Average coin silver content (grammes)
Caracalla	211–17	26	4.3	3.4
Macrinus	217–18	1	1.0	3.4
Elagabalus	218–22	127	31.75	2.8
Sev. Alexander	222–35	6	0.42	1.25
Maximinus	235–38			1.1
Balbinus/		6	2.0	
Pupienus	238	68	68.00	2.0
Gordian III	238–44	8892	1498.60	2.0
Philip	244–49	6990	1398.00	1.8
Decius	249–51	2321	773.60	1.7
Gallus/				1.7
Volusian	251–53	1401	467.00	1.2
Aemilian	253	52	52.00	1.2
Valerian/				
Gallienus	253–60	858	122.50	1.0

Table D

which pastoral farming is practised. Do we then have a record of hoard activity or a record of modern crop production? The discovery of hoards in upland areas by the use of metal detectors points to the latter conclusion and, until further research clarifies the picture, the archaeologist or historian would be well advised to use currently extant distribution maps with caution. Even greater caution should be used in accepting the locating of hoards by users of metal detectors who are not working in collaboration with established research groups. Provenances have been altered in order to avoid prosecution for operating illegally on scheduled monuments or to avoid the claims of landowners on whose property hoards have been discovered. The paths of scholarship and of profit diverge very rapidly indeed when the scent of 'buried treasure' is in the air.

CHAPTER FIVE

Coins and the site archaeologist
I

Because coins can be dated either very precisely, or within a very narrow time band, they have a pre-eminent place in the range of tools available to the archaeologist seeking to date his site or set it within a wider context of social and political events. Unfortunately, the way in which archaeologists have used, and are using, coin evidence is deplorable. Many discussions of sites are based on naïve and erroneous assumptions rising from a profound ignorance of the problems which are inherent in numismatic studies.

Coins hold a special place in the artefacts created by man because they are symbols of a range of absolutely fundamental activities. Coins are money: money buys food, clothing, shelter, security, pleasure. Hoarded coins may represent the savings of an individual to face an uncertain old age; individually, coins may be the difference between eating or starving. Coins are not wantonly discarded unless they cease to fulfil these minimal functions. They are certainly not lightly discarded for the benefit of archaeologists.

The poet Robert Herrick put the matter succinctly in the seventeenth century:

> When all birds else do of their music fail,
> Money's the still sweet-singing nightingale.

A pot once broken is, by and large, a useless object, its fragments to be discarded. But the broken pot can be replaced by the use of a coin which, after passing in the transaction for the new pot, will go on in other hands to fulfil another economic task. In many respects this makes the pot a more valuable archaeological object than the coin because it is common, of little value and used by virtually all members of the community. It is irreparable, useless when broken and, for all of these reasons, soon discarded. Unfortunately pottery is intrinsically undatable so that a very large part of the ceramic dating record depends on the ability to cross date pottery with coins. This situation may, however, shortly change with the development of intrinsic age determination methods for pottery, such as thermoluminescent dating. If there is sufficient refinement of these methods in the future it may well be that pottery will be used to date the deposit of associated coinage; but that day has not yet come so, in the meantime, the archaeologist must struggle with the present situation.

Although coins are normally very carefully treated in transactions and their loss is restricted by close supervision during the process of transfer from one owner to another, they do, nevertheless, get mislaid and lost. The way that losses occur are not random, and patterns can be discerned which are created by factors intrinsic to all coinages. What factors create or condition coin losses and how can these be interpreted to ensure that archaeologists do not draw false conclusions from them?

Let us deal with site finds, leaving the discussion of hoards for Chapter 4. There are a number of self-evident general factors which govern coin losses, each of which will be dealt with in turn:

1. Coin losses are proportional to the volume of coinage originally issued.

2. Coin losses are proportional to the intrinsic value of the coins issued.

3. Coin losses are proportional to political factors prevailing during the lifetime of coins.

4. Coin losses are proportional to economic factors prevailing during the lifetime of coins.

To these may be added a further factor which has a feature of variability that takes it out of the generalised categories above:

5. Coin losses are frequently proportional to the physical size of individual coins in the original coin population.

1. Coin losses are proportional to the volume of coinage originally issued

We have already seen that even in relatively sophisticated coin-using economies, like that of the Roman empire, the production of coin is at a variable rate both over long periods of time and from year to year. Clearly a period of high coin output will leave more evidence, in the form of its products, than a low output period. It is useless to compare, say, the coinage of the Roman period with that of the Merovingian because the coinage of the former is prolific and the coinage of the latter relatively scarce. They are not the same thing at all. Similarly, within a single coinage system there will be abundant years and less abundant years and the former will be better represented in the coin record than the latter. In short, there is a bias introduced by the production cycle which must affect the interpretation of the coin evidence by the archaeologist.

A simple model of this factor can be established from modern coinage. Figure 6 shows the results of plotting a random sample of modern coins against a record of the total numbers of the denomination issued. A sample of five pounds' worth of 2-pence pieces was obtained from a bank and sorted by date of issue, the number of coins for each date plotted against the Royal Mint's production figures for the period covered by the sample. As might be expected, years in which high numbers of coins were struck show up better in the sample than years in which fewer coins were produced. At some future date, were nothing but the coin evidence available, the numismatic evidence derived from coins coming from this sample would inevitably cluster round the years 1971, 1979, 1980 and 1981, with the chance of a 1971 date being overwhelming for the foreseeable future simply because there is a much greater chance of any coin lost from the sample being of this date.

Unfortunately, for most periods we have no convenient documentary records of coin output and other methods have to be resorted to in order to establish the sort of pattern revealed by the mint records. As will be seen there are ways of establishing coin patterns which permit an estimation of the dominance of some coins in the record and the scarcity of others.

2. Coin losses are proportional to the intrinsic value of the coins issued

This proposition can be summed up as 'the search for factor'. The degree of effort that goes into the recovery of a lost coin is directly related to its intrinsic or fiduciary value. In a coin population of mixed denominations it is the lowest value coins which people can best afford

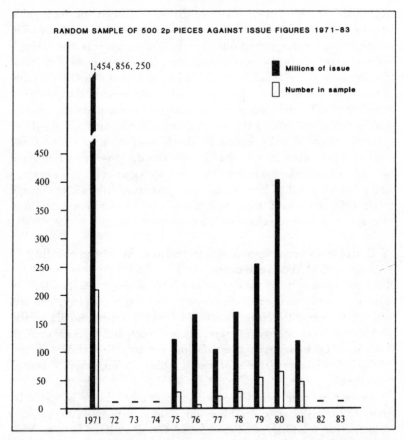

RANDOM SAMPLE OF 500 2p PIECES AGAINST ISSUE FIGURES 1971-83

6. Sample of two pence pieces withdrawn from circulation compared to issue figures.

to lose and on which they will expend the least effort of recovery. The treatment of the recently demonetised ½-pence coin exemplifies the principle. Here we have a denomination which was of such low value that it was seen discarded on the floors of supermarkets or in the gutters of the streets. On the other hand, pound coins are not treated in this manner. They are both very much worth recovering and relatively less common in the current coin population.

Exactly the same principles cover the loss of coins in the past. In general, site finds of coins are of the very lowest denominations. They are, in short, junk coins. Of course disasters happen and high value coins are lost from time to time, but these losses are inconsequential in relation to lower denominations. A complicating factor is that the high value coins of one period may become the low value coins of later years. For instance, the *sestertius* in the first century AD was a fairly high value coin and most losses of the period consist of copper *asses*, the quarter of the *sestertius*. By the second century *sestertii* are much more common and in the third century the losses of base metal coins are mostly of *sestertii*, often of ones issued in the second century. Over these centuries prices had risen so that the effective day-to-day currency had shifted to a silver based system and the high value coins of a previous age were relegated to low value status. Eventually the silver coinage itself suffered the same fate and losses of silver occur in proportion to the large numbers released into the currency pool.

3. Coin losses are proportional to political factors prevailing during the lifetime of coins

Political factors must figure prominently in any consideration of coinage since coins themselves are an expression of collective political will on the part of the issuing state. To detect the operation of political factors in the volume of coinage is not always easy but there are enough instances of coin deposit patterns being directly influenced by strictly political decisions to make it certain that an important factor is operative.

An extreme case would be where a national currency is ousted by that of an invasive state. In this event, unless the ousted coinage has a remelt value, it is likely to be abandoned, forming a large component of the residual numismatic record. Such events are rare but the imposition of a new political allegiance may result in the need to change the metrological basis of a coinage to conform with the standard of the dominant state. It was for this reason that the cities of Greece that came under Athenian domination changed the standard of their coinage to conform with that of Athens with whom they were, by force, attached by political and economic links. In Spain new monetary standards were adopted by the Iberian tribes brought under Roman domination in the third century BC. Events such as these should be detectable in the coin record and signal to the problem orientated archaeologist. More easily detected are deposits created by policies of demonetisation of coinage for economic reasons, or the condemnation of rival political factions. The tradition of *damnatio memoriae* has already been discussed (*Chapter 2*) but it is worth reiterating that it may result in the deposit of very large numbers of coins, as in the case of the coinage of Carausius, or conversely in the survival of very few coins, as resulted from the melting down of the coinage of Caligula.

Misguided governmental economic decisions are, of course, not unknown, and such decisions may result in marked influences on coin deposits. Few such decisions can have had such a profound effect on the coinage of a nation as that of the British government in the second half of the eighteenth century. A mistaken economic theory relentlessly pursued, in fact a failure to appreciate that the circulation of coin is not a drain on the resources of the state but a means of creating wealth, resulted in the decision to issue virtually no copper or silver coinage between the accession of George III and 1806. The resulting coin pattern is one which, in the absence of historical knowledge of the period, could be interpreted as one indicating a long economic crisis instead of an industrial revolution, overseas expansion and profound social change. We cannot expect records of events as well known as those of the eighteenth century to survive for ever and a numismatic interpretation of the period at some unimaginable future date might follow the line of reasoning expressed above. Records for most periods of human activity have vanished and we ourselves are now the unimaginable future of the Greeks, the Romans or the Carolingians. It is worth bearing in mind that they too may have behaved irrationally or from profoundly mistaken premises.

4. Coin losses are proportional to economic factors prevailing during the lifetime of coins

We can divide this proposition into a number of separate factors. Dizzying inflation may result in a vast increase in the numbers of coins in circulation whilst a deflation, or currency reform, may result in a severe restriction in the number of coins in circulation. At the level of the individual site there may be a selective operation of economic factors, with some centres of activity participating in coin use and others being restricted. For instance, military sites may produce coins because the troops participate in a cash based economy. These troops may be stationed in a zone which either does not participate in that economy from choice or is not allowed to participate for economic or other reasons.

Our final category of generalisation calls attention to physical factors.

5. Coin losses are frequently proportional to the physical size of individual coins in coin population

The caveat in this axiom is important because, although it is generally true that large coins are more easily recovered when lost than small coins, the changing value of large coins over the lifespan of a currency system may, despite their bulk, so reduce their monetary value as to make the hot pursuit of the individual large sized lost coin hardly worth the trouble. As a rule the value of a coin is related to its size. In precious metal denominations the weight of metal obviously related to the value of the coin, less metal giving less value. Within limits the same applies to base metal issues. For obvious reasons higher values are more acceptable if they have an enhanced size; witness the odium which attaches to the 20-pence coin which is smaller than its fraction the 5-pence piece. Coin losses will be determined by these factors: the visibility of the coin (size), the value of the coin (metal) and the proportion of the denominations that make up the currency. Higher value coins contain more currency units so that fewer coins are needed per transaction. Lower value coins will be issued in greater numbers because more are needed to make up the sum of anything but the minimum transaction.

These factors do not exist as separate categories of restriction on the flow of coinage to the site; all interact to produce coin patterns which are specific to different currency systems, of different periods and types of site. Before considering the practical problems which this analysis raises in specific periods, coinages or sites, we must consider another series of factors which the archaeologist must bear in mind when using coin evidence.

The coin and its context

We start with what the archaeologist calls, in his jargon, the 'site formation record'. That is the final accumulation of material, both soil and artefacts, which make up the archaeological site and the manner in which it came to take the form in which it is presented to the excavator.

Just as the coin is the product of a series of events so the archaeological context in which it is found on the site will be the product of a series of natural and man-made events. The soil is disturbed by building activity, by naturally occurring erosion processes, by the activity of animals and by agriculture. Trees send their roots through archaeological strata, posts are dug down, foundation trenches excavated, material is dumped in levelling for building, and garbage is scattered to fill ditches and depressions. These are some of the factors which create the environment in which coins are found. In an ideal archaeological world coins would be dropped in convenient places and remain there undisturbed until disinterred by the excavator using the most refined techniques of recovery allied to a keen perception of numismatic problems and their solutions. In reality this hardly ever happens because of the disturbances which are outlined above, but occasionally a site, of a single period, appears which demonstrates the truth of the adage about the value of 'the right coin in the right place'.

The legionary fortress at Inchtuthil, in Perthshire, was constructed at the end of the campaigns of Gnaeus Julius Agricola, whose campaigns in Britain between AD 73 and 83 were intended to complete the conquest of Britain begun by the emperor Claudius in AD 43. The fortress, which was designed to hold a full legion of about 5,800 of the best troops in the army of Britain, would have been the pivotal point for the control of Scotland. Shortly after Agricola's departure from Britain, in AD 83, work on the fortress ceased and demolition of the nearly completed structure began.[1] The demolition was systematic, timbers were recovered from buildings and strategic materials buried to prevent them falling into enemy hands. In the pits and trenches dug by the demolition gangs to recover reusable timbers or to bury material valuable to the enemy, were freshly minted coins issued in AD 86. The uncirculated condition of these coins and the contexts in which they were found makes it possible to date within close limits the demolition of the fortress. By inference, the dating of the demolition of the pivotal army base also dates the abandonment of the attempt by the Romans to control the Highlands and, with this, the withdrawal from any attempt to pursue a policy for the conquest of the whole island of Britain. This decision, so eloquently testified to by the coin evidence, was to colour the whole subsequent history of Roman Britain and to initiate the political events which contributed to the destruction of the province in the fifth century.

On the whole, though, archaeological sites are multi-phase and it is in this context that coin evidence can best be considered. It does not follow that, once discarded, a coin will stay where it was dropped. The factors listed above ensure that the coin may well have a migratory life shifting from context to context with each intervention in the site formation process.

At its simplest a coin in a sealed context dates the deposition of all of the material stratified above it to a date later than the production of the coin. Thus a floor laid on top of a coin of, say, 1900 must have been laid later than the year in which the coin was produced; the coin provides a *terminus post quem* date for this event. The coin does not produce a date at which the floor was laid, only one *before* which the event could *not* have taken place. The time which may have elapsed between the production of the coin, its loss and the laying of the floor is not specified by the context. Each of these time lapses may have been long or short and the crucial problem is to resolve the chronology created by the presence of the coin into a more refined system. One way is to establish a longer stratified sequence in which coins later than our 1900 one occur in contexts which are stratigraphically later. In this case the coins would form a sequence and, in our hypothetical model, the next level of our site might contain coins of 1920 and the next above that issues of the 1940s. We would then have a series of coin dated events to which we could attach a series of date brackets:

> Phase 1 Uncertain date . . . Coin of 1900
> Phase 2 Later than 1900
> Phase 3 Later than 1920
> Phase 4 Later than 1940

A simple sequence such as this hardly ever exists in the real world of excavation. Two major factors militate against this ideal state: the residual nature of coins in the currency pool from which the losses are derived and the intrusion of residual coins redeposited from earlier contexts.

The problem of the residuality of coins in the currency pool will be dealt with shortly; in the meantime we can consider the problems which arise from disturbance of the site through the sorts of agencies outlined above. Figure 7 illustrates the situation found in the excavation of the Roman fort at Caernarvon, in North Wales. Instead of the neat chronological sandwich predicted in our hypothetical model, we find that early coins are stratified above later issues or intrude between deposits of coins of successive chronological periods. Our illustration is of the successive features excavated in the fort

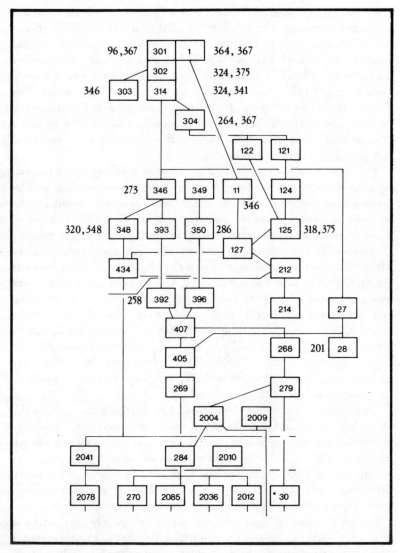

7. Caernarvon. Coin/feature matrix (the figures in the boxes are the identification numbers of individual features; those outside the boxes are the dates of the coins found in the corresponding features).

expressed as a matrix. Each numbered box in the matrix represents an individual archaeological feature: a post hole, wall, pit, floor or any other discontinuity. The relationship of the features to each other is shown by the vertical relationship of the features in the matrix. Features which are horizontally linked in time are pulled together by the connective lines of the matrix. We can see that there is a fixed physical relationship between the features and can assume that this relationship is also temporal. If we add to the features in the matrix the dates of the coins found in them, it becomes clear that, whilst there is a general gradient of dates from the lowest, or earliest, levels upwards, early coins appear in late contexts.

The coins found in redeposited or intrusive contexts may very well be extremely mixed in date, ranging over several centuries. The homogenous nature of the coinage in such deposits should not be accepted as evidence for the contemporaneity of use of such coins. They do not represent a currency horizon, only a taphonomic phase.

If we look at a case like that of the coins from the excavations at York Minster we can see how very varied the coinage can be in deposits associated with a site on which building activity has been constant over many centuries and where massive transformations of the stratified deposits have taken place. If we tabulate the coins found in the various layers stratified in the headquarters building of the Roman legionary fortress, underlying the medieval church, which was founded in the late 70s AD and abandoned by the Roman army probably in the early fifth century, we find that coins of all periods are represented even in the latest period (*see Table E*).

Clearly there is no very close correlation between the coins in the individual phases and the dates arrived at by considerations of relative archaeological stratigraphy and pottery studies. But the overall distribution of coins through time gives a good general view of activity on the site from the Flavian period to the fourth century, despite the ultimate mixing of the coins and their deposition in later contexts than those in which they may originally have been dropped.

Inevitably there will be occasions when a completely false situation will arise and a mixed population of redeposited coins present a convincing picture of activity which is unrelated to what really happened on the site. Once again, the York excavation provides us with a salutary reminder of the fallibility of all archaeological evidence.

In the complex of buildings which was found in the area of the

York Principia		
Phase	Coins and issue dates	Archaeological dating
1. Timber building	No coins	Flavian, 70s AD——→
2. First stone HQ	No coins	? Trajanic——→
3. Floor make-up	Republic 91 BC Vespasian AD 71 Domitian AD 86 Nerva AD 97 Tetricus I AD 270–3	Early 4th century——→
4a. Floor make-up	Antoninus Pius AD 153–4 Caracalla AD 212–18	Later 4th century——→
4b. Activity in Basilica	Marcus Aurelius 161–80 Gallienus 266–68 Victorinus 268–70 Tetricus II 270–73 Claudius II 27 Constantius II 330–35	Later 4th century
5. Post-Roman use for industry?	'Tetricus II' 273 + 'Constantine I' 341–6 Constans 346–8 Valentinian I 364–75	
6. Demolition	Marcus Aurelius 176–7	Prob. c.800–850

Table E

legionary fortress's headquarters were parts of the barracks of the First Cohort. Part of this building complex had a timber phase which yielded a series of coins of the second half of the third century in the proportions which would be characteristic of the sort of pattern expected in a late third-century context. As such they appear to date the building to the last decades of the third century or the first years of the fourth – both periods when intensive military activity is attested in the north of Britain. But close examination of the stratigraphical context of the building shows clearly that it was of post-Roman date and that the coins had been inadvertently incorporated in the structure by its Anglian builders who had derived building materials and soil from an earlier deposit.

CHAPTER SIX

Coins and the site archaeologist
II

A problem which exercises everyone who deals with coins as archaeological finds is why are there so many of them? A Roman excavation of any size can expect to produce several hundred coins, and archaeologists working on Mediterranean sites must cope with enormous numbers of Hellenistic, Roman and Arab issues. Were people in the past simply careless or is there some operative factor which affects the loss of coins?

We have seen that there are a number of factors external to the coinage itself which can help to create the site coin record. A further one, which is very important, is that the environment in which the coin is lost may influence the chances of receovery by the loser. Ignoring contexts like rivers and wells, which by their nature make recovery virtually impossible, we can suggest a number of environments in which the chances of recovering a dropped coin would be diminished. Muddy, unpaved areas into which coins could be trampled offer an immediate bonus to the archaeologist, but well-tended buildings, either public or private, with paved or hard floors present a less receptive environment from the point of view of dropped coins remaining in a situation which will aid the archaeologist. In fact, coins which are associated with floors are often those which have fallen through gaps in long vanished floor boards or have been stored in the rafters and have fallen to the floor in the collapse of the building. In neither case do such coins offer a good numismatic date for the construction phase of the building in question.

We can also speculate about the sorts of places in which coins are used, or carried. On the whole one does not expect a lot of coins to be used in the home, and farmers do not need to carry coins with them when they plough their fields or milk their cows. On the other hand, the market should be the place where a great deal of coin changes hands, especially the minor denominations which are most used in small transactions or given in change and which conform to the class of coinage which we have defined as being that which people can best afford to lose. Good markets operate in an anarchic atmosphere of bustle and excitement and amid heaps of discarded cabbage leaves, rotting fruit, jettisoned wrappers and general commercial detritus; just the sort of place, in fact, where coins would be lost and difficult to recover.

The excavation of the market place of ancient Athens, the Agora, illustrates the point well.[1] Of the 13,924 coins recovered spanning the first century BC to the end of the fifth century AD, only 178 (1.28 per cent) were of silver. All the rest were copper, bronze or billon (bronze with a tiny addition of silver) minor denominations and there were no gold coins at all.

At Verulamium (St Albans) a similar situation was found.[2] The market place once again produced large numbers of coins but they were not found in the immediate environs of the market building and its surrounding stalls because the market itself was swept up after the day's trading and the rubbish carted off to a nearby dump. In this case the dump was the town's abandoned theatre which was nearby, from which the Muses had been evicted and the cult of Cloaca installed in their place.

Other locations which produce large numbers of coins are religious sites and the civilian settlements found outside military installations. The practice of devoting coins in offerings at temples, churches and shrines is as old as coinage itself. The first recognisable coin hoard is that incorporated in the foundation of the temple of Diana at Ephesus and a steady stream of offerings of individual coins can be found in most religious sites. Even the Christian Church has not stamped out the practice, as the contents of the grave of Childeric, the Frankish king buried in Tournai cathedral in AD 482 shows. In modern times coins occur in graves as late as the seventeenth century and the practice of devoting coins at quasi-religious sites can still be found in parts of rural Ireland. A consideration of the problems which pertain to coin finds from religious sites would not be out of place.

In comparing site coin lists with each other we should always strive to compare like with like. Care must be taken to exclude any class of site which is incompatible with any other. Thus to compare a fort with a town is not proper because, by their nature, they will have experienced very different monetary regimes. Temples present a specific problem in this regard because the coins deposited there are not lost but deliberately deposited. The donor chooses the denomination of his gift and this may reflect his wealth, the degree of anxiety or gratitude felt, or the practices of the particular temple, shrine or church. Coins found in these circumstances are not the result of random events and they do not represent the picture of a currency subject to the normal vicissitudes of a circulating coinage. More importantly, coins left as votive deposits are not very likely to be removed from their place of deposit because they have been sanctified by their location. The result is that such coins will not accurately reflect changes in the coinage in the same way that sites within a dynamic coin system will reflect changes in denominational structure and type frequency. Votive deposits will preserve good coinage or the sort withdrawn by economic pressure in normal circumstances. Such sites are likely to show a higher incidence of better coinage and return high scores of actual coin units for periods when low scores are found on non-religious sites.

Military stations in the ancient world were places from which an injection of coinage into the regional economies took place and, as such, were a powerful magnet to civilian settlement. Where such settlements existed, the pay of the soldiers might be expected to drain from the camp into the extra-mural commercial establishments, through commercial transactions or because the dependants of the soldiers lived in the settlement and were maintained by the regular pay of the soliders.

Although we can observe contexts in which what appear to be large numbers of coins are lost, with the exception of the religious sites it is difficult to explain exactly why these losses occur. Pockets are a fairly recent addition to clothing. In most periods and cultures people carried their money in purses which range from simple cloth or leather bags to the complicated lidded purses of the medieval period. Perhaps, though, the problem is being looked at in the wrong way: we should not ask 'why were so many coins lost?' but 'why was so little money lost?'.

The archaeologist, possibly overwhelmed with his haul of coins, may see them only in the context of his own site and not in the wider framework of the economic situation in which they were produced. Even very large numbers of coins from site finds usually represent very little in terms of real money, and even less when it is remembered that the losses are often spread over several centuries. One way in which we can put the problem into perspective is to look at the coins from a single site for which we can make a reasonable projection of what fraction they are of a calculable original coin population. We can do this by looking at the coins from a Roman fort site where we have information about the composition of the garrison. The history of the fort at Corbridge has been elucidated by nearly a century of excavation.[3] This work has established that from the first century to the second half of the second century it was garrisoned by a succession of regiments of the Roman army (*see Table F*).

Date	Name	Composition
*c.*85–95	Ala Petriana	500-strong cavalry unit
*c.*95–*c.*105	?	?1000-strong mixed infantry
*c.*106–*c.*118	?	1000-strong mixed cavalry and infantry unit
*c.*118–*c.*125	?	1000-strong infantry unit
*c.*125–*c.*138	Ungarrisoned	
*c.*138–*c.*154	?	?500-strong cavalry unit
*c.*154–*c.*163	Cohors I Vardullorum	1000-strong mixed cavalry and infantry unit

Table F

During this occupation the pay rates for troops were stable. Auxiliary infantry men in cohorts were paid a basic 100 *denarii* a year. Cavalrymen in *alae* received 200 *denarii* and those serving in the mixed cavalry/infantry units drew 150 *denarii*, their unmounted colleagues being paid the same rate as soldiers in a regular infantry unit. Of the units serving at Corbridge the regular *Cohors Quingennaria* consisted of 480 men, whilst a *Cohors Milliaria* held 960. The mixed units consisted of 800 infantry and 240 cavalrymen. From these figures we can calculate the annual total cost in pay of the various units (*see Table G*).

Our calculation of the total sum payable to the troops over this period is the very lowest level (that is, ignoring the higher salaries of

Period	Date	Men	Pay in denarii	Years in garrison	Total pay
I	85–95	480	200	10	960,000
II	95–105	960	100	10	960,000
III	106–118	800	100 ⎫	13	1,508,000
		240	150 ⎭		
IV	118–125	960	100	8	768,000
V	138–154	480	200	17	1,632,000
VI	154–163	800	100 ⎫	9	1,044,000
		240	150 ⎭		6,872,000 denarii

Table G

officers): the troops at Corbridge would have received at least 6,872,000 *denarii* in pay. The total number of coins recovered from this site for these years totals 1,387 coins, excluding the quite exceptional find of a hoard of *aurei*. This haul of coins consists of all denominations but, as might be expected, small denominations predominate. If the whole collection is expressed as a single denomination, the gold *aureus*, we find that the whole mass of coins amount to eight *aurei*. Eighty years of collection and eighty-odd years of losses amount to no more money that the annual pay of two of the lowest paid soldiers serving in the fort for two years. On the basis of the estimate of the total potential coin population of 274,880 *aurei* (one *aureus* = 25 *denarii*), we have recovered less than 0.003 per cent of this coinage with which to establish the date of a multitude of features representing eight decades of intensive activity, or to calculate the impact of troops on the economy of the area in which they served. Corbridge is a particularly favoured site because it has been subjected to such a great deal of investigation; most sites have not benefitted from such close scrutiny and the resulting coin totals are correspondingly small. We can visualise the problem on a larger scale by undertaking the same exercise that we have used to illustrate the problems of Corbridge for the legionary fortress of Caerleon. This fortress was the base of Legio II Augusta and the regiment consisted of some 5,500 men who were paid at a higher rate than the inferior, non-citizen, forces of the frontier fort. The minimum coin population of the site, to the first quarter of the third century, would amount to 374,012,500 *denarii* or 14,880,500 *aurei* of which we have a record of twelve and a half *aureus* worth (611 coins), or 0.000000334 percentage of the potential coin population.[4]

Faced with the problems raised by such elementary, rough statistical exercises as these conducted on relatively small sites with limited occupational histories, it would be well to reflect on the volume of coinage which must have circulated in the great cities of antiquity or the burgeoning mercantile towns of the Middle Ages. These towns and cities had large populations and a thousand years of economic activity conducted through the medium of coinage. All things are relative but in coin studies the relativity of the surviving coinage to the original volume of coins in circulation is minimal.

We have tried to illustrate the paucity of real money from the Roman period when the coinage is the chief dating aid and economic indicator. There are periods and societies in which coinage played a much less important role than it did in the Roman Empire. There are also instances where, because of the nature of the currency, the surviving material is very scarce. In societies which used a currency dominated by very high value coins, such as early Celtic tribal coinage, the volume of coin for study will be small and the treatment of such coinage for dating and elucidating sites proportionally restricted. The value of coinage to the archaeologist is often in inverse proportion to its intrinsic value – a collection of rubbish coins like those from Athens is of infinitely greater academic value than any single masterpiece of numismatic art. The volume of coinage can be restricted by other factors, such as its use by society in a very limited range of transactions or sheer poverty. Whatever the reason for the scarcity of coin the dearth created may inhibit the effects on the use of such coinage for site or feature dating. On the other hand, the occurrence of scarce coins can add enormous weight to the chronological, economic and political deductions which may be drawn by archaeologists. Frequently the periods which produce least coins are those which are the most obscure so that coins may offer an exceptional insight into otherwise impenetrable problems.

Such a case can be illustrated from the excavation of the Saxon ship found under a barrow at Sutton Hoo in Suffolk.[5] Native Saxon coinage does not appear in England before the middle of the sixth century and such transactions as took place through the medium of coin before this innovation seem to have been conducted through the use of coins imported from Merovingian Gaul, where a well-developed system existed, based upon the late Roman gold denominations. The Sutton

Hoo ship contained a hoard of Merovingian coins together with a number of gold blanks and billets. Argument still rages as to the significance of the coins in terms of their possible symbolic function in what is generally agreed to have been a Christianised funerary deposit – albeit a funerary deposit which may have been devoid of an actual corpse. Whatever the reason for the inclusion of the coins in the ship their numismatic history is clear and, as the latest datable objects in the deposit, they offer the archaeologist the best evidence available with which to date the burial. It does not need emphasising that to establish such a date would put into a chronological framework other objects included in the burial which are intrinsically undatable, such as the jewellery, domestic objects and artefacts which appear to be symbols of office or status. A further bonus must be accounted the important information about the development stage of the technology of boat building which is given by the remains of the burial ship itself. After decades of argument the consensus now is that the burial is numismatically established as being about AD 625, that being the date ascribed to the latest coins in the hoard. It is worth tracing the numismatic reasoning which led to this conclusion since it illustrates the manner in which the physical composition of coins can be used to establish a chronology.

The coinage of Merovingian Gaul underwent a series of debasements through the fifth and sixth centuries as supplies of precious metals dried up and Byzantine subsidies became less frequent. As a result the fineness of the gold coin declined in a number of recognisable stages. One steep descent in fineness took place in the years 625–30, but the Sutton Hoo collection contained no coin of the degree of debasement associated with this phase of the decline. The latest coins in the Sutton Hoo purse were of the standard which immediately preceded this stage, suggesting that they were assembled before the baser new coinage overwhelmed the coins of high intrinsic value of the previous generation. The metrology of the Merovingian coinage itself places a terminal date on the hoard. Normally such a date would serve as a *terminus post quem*, since the coins might be put into the ship at any date after 625, but the absence of coins later than this date on the new, baser, standard creates a *terminus ad quem*, a date before which an event must have taken place, if we accept the argument that such high standard coins would not have been available for hoarding soon after the issue of the lower value issues.

The notion that the absence of coins from an archaeological deposit is as important, or more important, as the presence of coins is one that must be stressed. Archaeology is not just about what is found, it is equally about what is not found. We have already mentioned the sorts of factors which create patterns of coinage: the problem of high denominations being badly represented, the periodicity of issue of coin and the factors governing the physical environment in which coins might be expected to be used and lost. Beyond these general factors are others which are specific to individual series of coins and to individual areas in which these series were used. The most closely studied of these systems is the coinage of Roman Britain and it is in this context that the factors influencing the use of coins by the archaeologist can be most easily discussed.

The investigation of numerous urban, rural and military sites in Britain has brought to light many thousands of coins which fall into a well-marked pattern. This pattern is characteristic of one corner of the Roman Empire; variations occur in other regions. Before discussing the pattern, and its important implications for the interpretation of coin evidence, we should look first at the external factors which help to contribute to its creation.

The sites chosen for this analysis are towns because these sites are, *ex hypotheosi*, unlikely to have suffered periodic depletion of their population in the same way that forts, with their shifting garrisons, are known to have suffered. We can postulate a fairly stable pattern of occupation, though not say that it was constant at all periods. However, we might expect most towns to have very much the same history of population growth and decline within the small area of urbanised Roman Britain.

We must, at the outset, notice that the material which is used in our survey has suffered discriminatory sorting at an early stage of its collection. Archaeologists tend to speak of 'stratified coins' and dismiss the other coins from a site as being of no interest. To make sense of a site in overall terms all of the coins associated with the site must be considered in this study; this means every coin found in excavation, no matter what its context, and every other coin ever found on the site. These may be casual finds donated to local museums, items found by metal detector users and still in private possession and items, now lost, which can be dug out of newspaper files or local histories. These coins must be individually identified with complete accuracy.

This is sometimes a difficult undertaking. Coins from excavations are frequently both very worn and very corroded, whilst coins in old records, or even respectable excavation reports, are often inadequately described. Nevertheless, in order to minimise bias every coin must be subjected to the closest study.

Some coins will inevitably defeat even the most skilled attempts at identification and in some areas the number of such unidentifiable specimens will be higher than in others. Coins from loamy and chalky soils are generally well preserved but those from wet, humic and acid environments are often in extremely poor condition. In the north of Britain the soil is so unhelpful to the preservation of coins that a high proportion may have been lost to study. A similar problem is found in environments with a high salinity or where wind-borne sand abrades the coins. Thus we have a series of natural physical problems, and to these we can add a sample bias which arises from the impracticality of archaeologists reaching the early levels of a site on the same scale that they can examine the uppermost levels. If we are dealing with all the coin recovered from a site such as a town then we take into consideration the coinage collected by casual finds, field walking and systematic excavation. These processes will collect surface material which is overwhelmingly the coinage of the latest period so that we may have the coinage of many acres of the fourth century but of only a few square metres of the first-century landscape. At the best it can be claimed that the same problem is likely to be met on most sites with a consequent equalising effect on the sampling strategy over a large area of study.

The next problem is to ensure that we are comparing like with like. It is plainly foolish, though not an unknown occurrence, to look at a coin list and claim that, because some coins are found more frequently than others, there has been a change in the level of site activity reflected by the coins. Not only is this bad logic but manifestly wrong, since it takes no cognisance of the fact that the coins which make up the site list will have been issued over various lengths of time. Long reigns produce more coins than short; we cannot say that because there are more coins of Hadrian about than of Titus that there was more coin activity in the reign of the former than of the latter. Nonsense, all that is shown is that Hadrian reigned for twenty years and that Titus survived for only two years. What the student must do is eliminate the discrepancy created by the differing issue periods by expressing the coins in his comparative study as the product of individual regnal years. In this way the true underlying production trend can be established. To do this we divide the total coinage for each reign, or currency issue period, by the length of time over which the coins were issued. This is a fairly rough and ready method of equalisation but one which works in practice very well, though it ignores the unevenness of coin issue even within very short periods, which we have already noted as a characteristic of all coinage regimes.

Next we need to ensure that site by site comparison is also on a like with like basis, because different sites will produce different volumes of coin, either for the exploratory reasons outlined above or because of the size of the site itself. Comparison can be made only if the coins are put on a common numerical basis. In practice it has been found that expressing total coin population of a site as 1000 coins gives a good statistical base.[6] This is achieved by dividing the total of coins for the site *by* a thousand, if the total is greater than a thousand coins, and *into* a thousand if the total is smaller. The resulting figure is then used as a multiple for each component of the list. For example, if we have 1500 coins from a site then by multiplying the coins of each reign/period by 0.67 (i.e. $\frac{1000}{1500} = 0.67$) we will have all of our coins expressed as so many per thousand. Assuming twenty of the total are Hadrianic, then there are 20×0.67 ($= 13.4$) Hadrianic coins per thousand of site total. But another step must be taken if we are to compare the Hadrianic coinage with any other period. We must ascertain the yearly rate of representation and divide our 13.4 coins by the twenty years of his reign. So $\frac{13.4}{20} = 0.67$ (annual average coin loss).

The two elements of the equalising process can be brought together into a simple and self-explanatory formula:

$$\frac{\text{number of coins per reign or issue period}}{\text{length of reign or issue period}} \times \frac{\text{site coin total}}{1000} = \begin{array}{l}\text{annual} \\ \text{average} \\ \text{coin loss}\end{array}$$

This formula works very well for sites with more than 200 coins; below this figure distortions appear, created by the fact that the smaller the number of coins in the list the less well represented will be scarcer or rarer issues, and the greater will be the mathematical effects of the chance presence of material from periods normally lightly represented. Nevertheless, a comparison between quite disparate numbers of coins is very instructive because of the very strongly marked pattern which emerges when we express the numerical results achieved by application of the equalisation formula in a graphical form. The best form is a histogram, rather than a distribution curve, in which the density of coinage is expressed over a time scale. Figures 8–11 show the results of plotting the total coinage recovered, or recorded, from a series of sites in Britain. In this study the coin periods have been defined as shown in Table H.

Period	Date range	Principal rulers
1 Claudian	43–54	Claudius
2 Neronian	54–68	Nero
3 Flavian I	68–81	Vespasian, Titus
4 Flavian II	81–96	Domitian
5 Trajanic	96–117	Nerva, Trajan
6 Hadrianic	117–38	Hadrian
7 Antonine I	138–61	Antoninus Pius
8 Antonine II	161–80	Marcus Aurelius
9 Antonine III	180–92	Commodus
10 Severan I	193–217	Septimus Severus, Caracalla
11–17 Severan II	217–60	Elagabalus, Severus Alexander, Maximinus, Gordian III, Philip, Decius, Gallus, Valerian
18 Gallic Empire	260–73	Postumus, Victorinus, Tetricus, Gallienus
19 Aurelianic	273–86	Aurelian, Tacitus, Probus, Carinus
20 Carausian	286–96	Carausius, Allectus
21 Diocletianic	296–317	Diocletian, Maximian, Constantius, Galerius, Constantine I
22 Constantinian I	317–30	Constantine I, Licinius
23 Constantinian II	330–48	Constantine I, Constantine II, Constans, Constantius II
24 Constantinian III	348–64	Constantius II, Magnentius, Julian
25 Valentinianic	364–78	Valentinian I, Valens, Gratian
26 Theodosian I	378–88	Gratian, Theodosius I, Magnus Maximus
27 Theodosian II	388–402	Theodosius I, Honorius, Arcadius

Table H

In examining the resulting plots it is clear that there is a very strongly marked similarity between the sites (*Figures 8–11*). From this we can deduce that something other than the activity on the individual site must be influencing the resulting distribution diagrams, unless we

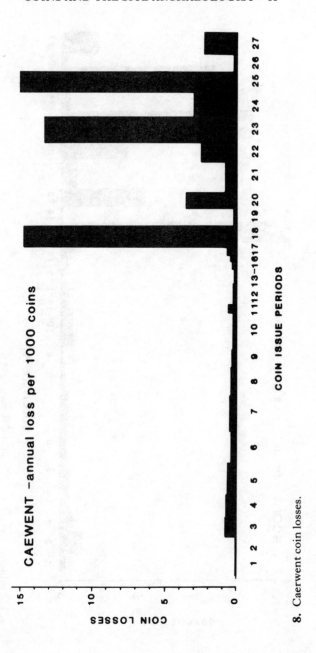

8. Caerwent coin losses.

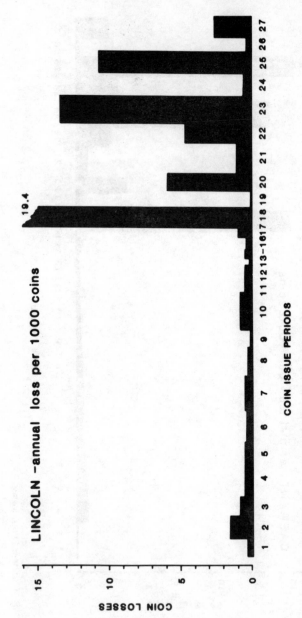

9. Lincoln coin losses (after Mann and Reece, 1983).

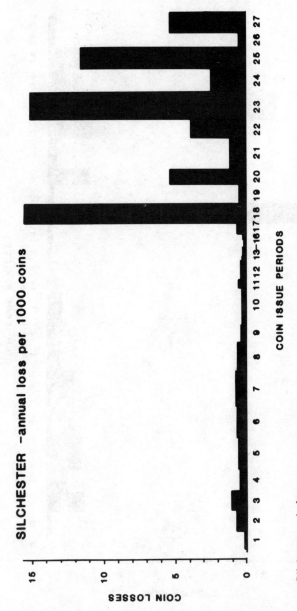

10. Silchester coin losses.

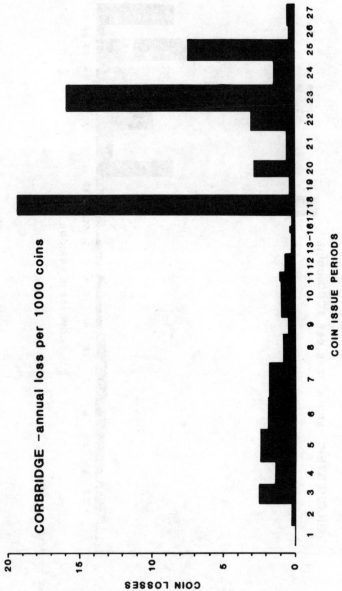

11. Corbridge coin losses.

are to postulate that exactly the same, non-numismatic, events took place at the same time and with the same intensity in very widely dispersed sites. This seems to be inherently unlikely, although we must not forget that widespread disasters do happen and that the Black Death had widespread effects in towns in fourteenth-century England. But recurrent events, as might be postulated from the histograms, can be confidently discounted. There is a factor in operation which is independent of the site and this factor lies in the nature of the coinage and currency found on the sites.

Before discussing what these factors might have been we shall consider the way in which the pattern has been interpreted by archaeologists who have based their work on observations drawn from individual sites, rather than from a wider context. The individual archaeologist often sees the site on which he has lavished a large part of his professional life as the centre òf some historical universe. All else is related to, measured by, and subordinated to it; Galileo probably had an easier time persuading the doubters that the earth was orbital to the sun than one has persuading an archaeologist that his site is not uniquely at the centre of past events. It is not surprising then that the interpretation of coins should suffer from particularism. A typical line of reasoning, and individual site interpretations will be examined later, explaining the distribution pattern shown in Figures 8–11 might run as follows.

The histogram shows that, after a slow start, site activity (?population) built up steadily to the third quarter of the second century. At that point a recession (?abandonment) took place and activity was at a very low level until the middle of the third century. At this time a sudden influx of people took place, the economy revived, and lots of coins were thrown around in a wild celebration of affluence. Unfortunately this gesture was premature and resulted in another crisis. This was again weathered and a prosperous period set in in the early decades of the fourth century. Again a retributive crisis set in which was overcome in the 360s, and after that came a steady downhill process culminating in an end of Roman administration in Britain. This interpretative scheme can, of course, be supported by historical evidence – itself derived perhaps from coin evidence – and so another historical myth will join the many others that proliferate in the archaeological textbooks.

It can be stated categorically that any such interpretation is wrong if it does not take into consideration the evidence from a range of sites. It may well be that individual sites could have suffered any number of problems: the economy may have been blighted, the population risen or fallen and that population may have lived in extraordinary squalor throwing their coins around with mad abandon during times of prosperity. But none of this is evidenced by the coins. What they show are changes in the nature of the currency, and the presence or absence of coins on these long occupied sites is determined by an economic or political situation which was the product not of individuals and individual sites but of policies pursued by a central government, itself pressured by social, economic and military events.

How should we see the features of the histograms if not as the result of individual site histories? When we break the component parts of the display down into the individual elements which make up the whole a number of features become clear. Firstly, the coinage of any one period is not the same as any other in terms of the mix of coins of which it is composed. The denominational weight changes from time to time; generally higher denominations are present in larger proportions as time passes. We could look at things in these terms, pointing out that the decline in the volume of coin from the later second century coincides with a change to an almost exclusively silver based system. A change to a silver coinage has the effect of reducing the number of coins available to be lost because each silver coin is the equivalent of several base metal ones and it is units of coinage in circulation which determine how many may be lost. Because the higher value losses are multiples of the base metal coinage there may be just as much money used on the site, though less lost. The state may have issued no less money and the inhabitants of the site in Roman Britain handle no less money than formerly, but it was issued and used in a different form. In fact there may be more money in circulation. Table I shows the coinage of a typical urban site expressed in terms of *asses* from the first century to the Severan period. As the coinage changes to silver in the late second century the volume of money lost actually rises as the number of units lost declines.

Clearly a system which operates on the sort of international scale as the Roman coinage will have a heavy masking effect on individual sites, and the detection of changes in site status through the medium of coins will be very difficult. The situation becomes worse as the third century progresses and gives way to the fourth. By this period the silver

PLATE 1

Salt bar. These bars were used in Abyssinia as the normal currency over extensive areas. European records first note their use in the sixteenth century, and they were still extant on the outbreak of the Second World War. The value of the unit of currency varied with the distance from the source of rock salt and the size of the bar. (Copyright the Museum of Mankind)

PLATE 2

1. 'Otho'. *Sestertius* created by Giovanni Cavino (Padua 1499–1570)

2. Leyden. During the Spanish siege in 1574, coins of 5, 10 and 20 stuivers were issued struck on the vellum leaves of prayer books and bibles.

3. Olbia. Bronze 'dolphin', third-century BC

4. Persian Asia Minor *c.*340 BC. Silver *tetradrachm* issued shortly before the campaigns of conquest of Alexander the Great. The anepegraphic obverse shows the Persian king in the traditional kneeling position drawing the reflex bow of his nomadic ancestors.

5(1) Alexander the Great (336–23 BC). Silver *tetradrachm*. Minted at Amphipolis. This specimen was struck during Alexander's lifetime. Early issues of this long lived type show the seated figure of Zeus with his legs side by side. Later issues depict the god in a more relaxed pose with the right leg poised on the toes behind the left. (British Museum Coll.)

5(2) 'Alexander the Great'. Silver *tetradrachm*. Mint of Odessos. Struck in the first century BC by Mithradates VI, king of Pontus. (British Museum Coll.)

6. Maria Theresia (1740–80). Silver *thaler*. Although dated 1780 this specimen was struck by the Vienna mint in 1980.

7. Ionia or Lydia. Electrum quarter stater, seventh-century BC. (British Museum Coll.)

8(1) Ceylon. Copy of Constantinian billon coinage. Fourth–fifth century AD. (British Museum Coll.)

8(2) Constantinian prototype of Ceylonese coinage.

9. Parthia. Parthamaspates (*c.*116). Silver *drachm*. This coin was issued by the puppet king placed on the Parthian throne by Trajan after his conquests of Persian territory beyond the Euphrates.

Coins shown slightly smaller than original size

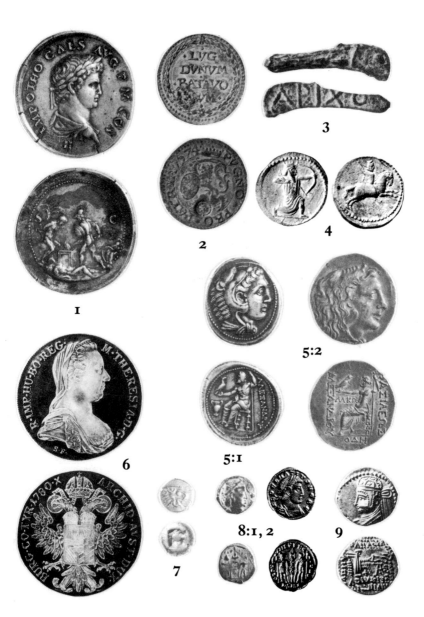

PLATE 3

1. Charles I. Silver pound minted at Oxford in 1644. (British Museum Coll.)

2. Antiochus VI. (145–42 BC). Silver *tetradrachm*. The Syrian king assumes the rays of divinity as well as the temporal diadem of the Hellenistic monarchs. The reverse inscription proclaims that he is 'Dionysus made Manifest'. This protective screen of divinity did not prevent his assassination by the regent Tryphon. (British Museum Coll.)

3. Maximianus Herculeus (286–305). The emperor carries the club of Hercules symbolising his constitutional position in relation to his senior colleague, Diocletian. The reputation of Hercules for clearing up tricky problems whilst engaged on his labours is assimilated into the function and imagery of the emperor.

4. John II Comnenus (1118–43). Gold *hyperperon*. The Virgin Mary crowns the emperor.

5. Alexius I Comnenus (1081–1118). Silver *trachy*. Saint Demetrius, the patron saint of Thessalonica where the coin was struck, holds the cross with the emperor. The saint's superior status to the emperor is indicated by his hand being higher up the cross shaft.

6. Christian Ludwig of Luneburg (1641–65). Silver multiple *thaler*. The divine hand crowns the emblem of the state and endorses the mining activity which produced the wealth from which the coin was produced. (British Museum Coll.)

Coins shown slightly smaller than original size

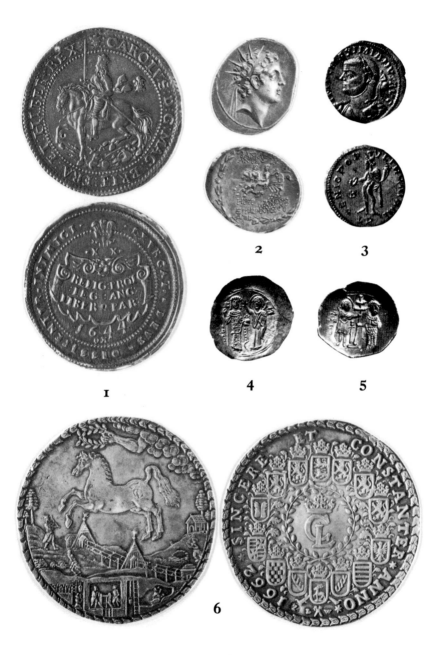

1

2

3

4

5

6

PLATE 4

1. Elizabeth II. Fifty-pence piece issued to celebrate Britain's accession to the EEC.

2. Justin II (565–78). Gold *solidus*. DOC. 4.

3. Nero (54–68). *Dupondius*. RIC 281 (British Museum Coll.)

4. Faustina I, posthumus (after 141). *As/Dupondius* RIC 1168. The coin shows the cult statue of the deified wife of Antoninus Pius within the memorial temple erected after her deification. (British Museum Coll.)

5. Caracalla (196-217), AE 26 of Isaura (Cilicia). The bust of Zeus is depicted as it stood in an aedicule within the temple.

6. Septimius Severus (193-211). Copper coin depicting the temple of Jupiter Heliopolitanus at Baalbek. (British Museum Coll.)

7. Philip I (244–49). Copper coin depicting the entrance to the temple complex. (British Museum Coll.)

Scale 1 : 1

1

3

2

4

5   6   7

PLATE 5

1. Septimius Severus and Geta. Copper coin of Stratonicaea (Cilicia). After his death at the hand of his brother, Caracalla, effigies of Geta were destroyed and his portrait chiselled off coins on which he appeared with his father or brother. (British Museum Coll.)

2. Nero and Vespasian. Caesaraea (Palestine). Vespasian was proclaimed emperor in Palestine in 69. His troops, especially Legio X Fretensis, produced an acceptable coinage for the new reign by hammering flat coins of Nero, now subject to *damnatio*, and countermarking them with a small punched portrait of Vespasian.

3. Gordian I Africanus (April 258). *Sestertius*. The short lived revolt of Gordian against Maximinus (235–38) evoked a coinage from the mint of Rome. This specimen has been defaced in antiquity following the collapse of the revolt.

4. Carausius (286–93). Silver *'denarius'*. Carausius, the usurper in Britain, is depicted in the ceremonial robes of a consul, a position he appointed himself to in 297. The coin would have been issued to celebrate this self-conferred honour as a gift to his army and administration.

5. Constantine I (305–37). Billon? 25-*denarius*. Mint of Siscia, 318.

6. Constans (337–50). Billon half *maiorina*. Mint of Heraclea, 348.

7. Andronikos II and Michael IX (1295–1320). Gold *hyperperon*. Fourteen carat standard. Virgin *orans* within six towered walls of Constantinople.

8. Andronikos II and Michael IX (1295–1320). Gold *hyperperon*. Twelve carat standard. Virgin *orans* within four towered walls of Constantinople.

9. Constantius II (337–61). Silver *miliarense*. The obverse depicts the emperor with his head raised in prayer, a conceit devised by his father Constantine which excited contemporary comment.

Scale 1 : 1

1

2

3

4

5

6

7

8

9

PLATE 6

1. Antoninus Pius (138–61). Copper *as*. Britannia seated.

2. Probus (276–82). Billon '*antoninianus*' Rome mint. The issue was produced as part of the ceremonies attending the visit of the emperor to the capital in 281.

3. Magnus Maximus (383–88). Gold *solidus*. London mint *c.*384. The mint mark indicates production at AVG (usta) the name bestowed on London in the fourth century. OB (bryzicum) indicates that the coin was struck from refined gold at the imperial court mint. (British Museum Coll.)

4. Philip II of Macedon (359–36). Gold *stater*. This coin, or a later Greek issue of the same type, is antecedent to much of the coinage of the western Celtic tribes and kingdoms.

5. Celtic-British. Gold *stater*. First century BC. The head of Apollo is still recognisable but the chariot of the original has been disintegrated and reintegrated through a series of transpositions in the intermediate coinages from which the present example ultimately derives.

6. Balbinus (258). *Sestertius* RIC. 19 and cliché mould.

7. Justinian (527–65) Copper *Follis*

8. Foil squeeze of coin no. 7

1

2

3

4

5

6

7

8

PLATE 7

1. Dies. The dies illustrated are the modern replicas of a set of Greek bronze dies used in David Sellwood's experimental striking of Greek silver tetradrachms.

2. Coin flan. Prepared but unused flan for the production of an Indo-Greek copper coin similar to that of Lysias (*c.*145–35 BC).

3. Field marks. Ptolemy I as satrap of Egypt under Alexander the Great. Silver tetradrachm. The reverse bears the name of Alexander, a figure of Pallas Athene accompanied by the eagle of Zeus. The Greek helmet below Athena's shield and the monogram by her leg are control marks which indicate the emission sequence and, probably, the name of the responsible official.

4. Denarius of the moneyer M. Furius Filus struck in 119 BC as a brockage.

I

2

3

4

PLATE 8

1. Galeria Valeria (wife of Galerius, 305–11). Billon *'follis'*. The mint mark can be expanded to *S(acra) M(oneta) T(hesalonicae) (Officina) A*.

2. Elizabeth II. Penny 1965.

3. Aethelred II (978–1016). Silver penny. Moneyer Aethered, minted in London (ÆTHERED MO LUND).

4. Edward I (1272–1307). Silver penny. Minted in Durham (CIVITAS DUREM).

5. 'Constantius II'. Copy of the *Fel Temp Reparatio* coinage of the period 354–60 overstruck on a Constantinian coin of 330–35.

6. Constantius II (337–61). *Fel Temp Reparatio* coin of *c*.354.

7. *Gloria Exercitus* undertype below *Fel Temp Reparatio* striking.

8. Constantine II, caesar (317–37). *Gloria Exerxitus* issue of 330–35.

9. Probus (276–82). Doublestruck billon *'antoninianus'*.

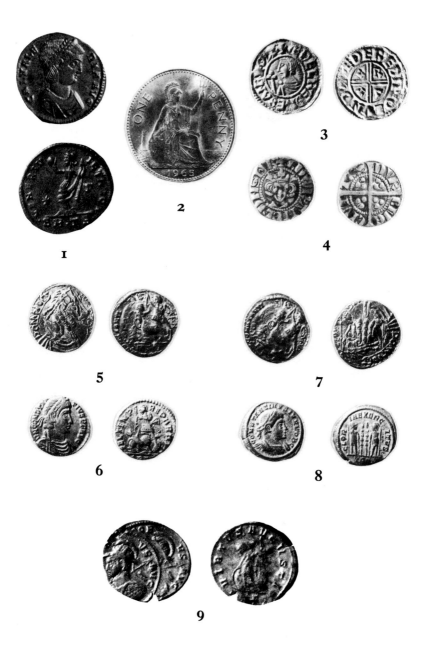

1

2

3

4

5

6

7

8

9

PLATE 9

Feather money. The island of Santa Cuz (Polynesia) developed this form of currency. The belt, up to 10m (33ft) long, is made up of the overlapping feathers of the Myzomela Cardinalis. Only the red feathers from the breast and around the eyes were used. About 400 to 600 birds contributed to the average belt. Feather money passed current in the purchase of ocean-going canoes, in bride price transactions and for the payment of the heavy fines imposed by the community for what missionary observers termed 'fornication'. (Copyright the Museum of Mankind)

| Issuer | Caerwent | |
	Coin units recovered	Annual monetary loss in asses
Claudius	1	0.02
Nero	4	0.3
Vespasian/Titus	38	11.0
Domitian	40	4.0
Trajan	47	9.5
Hadrian	29	6.0
Antoninus Pius	39	6.3
Marcus Aurelius	21	2.45
Commodus	14	5.0
Severus/Caracalla	20	10.7
Elagabalus	11	40.5
Severus Alexander	15	13.2

Table I

currency has been re-established but is not common in site finds which consist of very low value billon coins. The volume of the silver coinage is attested by its strong representation in hoards where it was the preferred medium for conserving wealth. The billon coins were periodically subjected to reforms or revaluations which temporarily created a dearth of coinage. Each of these reforms failed after a short period and the massive peaks of coinage in periods 23 and 25 represent the failure of the system to cope with inflation.

Paradoxically, the huge coin losses of the fourth century probably represent economic distress rather than prosperity. What is not evident from the graphs is any evidence of periodicity or density of occupation, or of economic activity which is specific to the individual site. It should not be overlooked that any serious economic or commercial activity would almost certainly be conducted through the medium of gold coinage and that, since this is virtually never found in site collections, we have absolutely no means of estimating the real level of an individual's financial activity in the Roman period from archaeologically recovered coin.

In this discussion we have explained the pattern of site finds in their financial aspects but coins are used for other purposes than speculative reconstructions of the economic situation. In these circumstances it would be wrong to dismiss periods with few coins, or none at all, as periods of low site activity or non-occupation if these periods are ones in which the coin deposit pattern is dictated by the nature of the coinage itself. Similarly the high coin activity periods cannot be seen, in simplistic terms, as a maximisation of occupation or other site activity.

In the light of these points let us look in detail at a recent excavation report and examine how the excavator's perception of the coins affects his interpretation of the site and its occupational sequence.

Figure 12 is a histogram produced for the coins excavated at the late Roman Saxon Shore fort at Portchester, Hampshire.[7] This site was constructed at the end of the third century, almost certainly by Carausius, and the coin distribution pattern reflects the absence of activity on the site before that period. A residual amount of coinage of the Gallic Empire (period 18) was still circulating at the moment of foundation. It may be noted that period 18 is relatively less strongly represented than on sites which flourished throughout the third century. Thereafter the relative strength of period to period representation is marked in a similar manner to other sites occupied throughout the fourth century. The ups and downs of the Portchester histogram are exactly comparable with those found in the graphical representation of the coins of all of the other sites (*Figures 8–11*). To interpret this site from its coins we need to consider the site within the overall context of the other sites. How does the exacavator see his site in isolation? In summary, two interpretations are offered. One, of a series of occupations and abandonments in which the equation is made that coin peaks mean occupation and troughs abandonment or diminished occupation. A second view is that the troughs are indicative of orderly occupation by clean-living troops and the peaks show the removal of the soldiers and their replacement by civilians who lived in a disorderly manner, hurling coins about, like penny throwers at a football match, with no regard for their value. This interpretation, of alternate civilian and military occupation, allows for further inferences about the strategy of defence in the fourth century and the periodicity of threats to Britain from external raiders, and the response of civilians, soldiers and the administration to these recurrent crises.

Seen in relation to other sites it is clear that what Portchester actually reflects, and it does so accurately, is the regular pattern of coinage in Britain at this period, and that the deductions made about

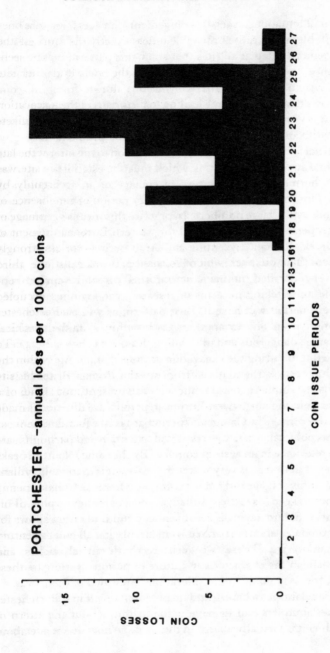

12. Portchester coin losses.

occupation fluctuations, social arrangements or local response to political problems are quite untenable unless exactly the same events could be demonstrated at all sites that show this pattern. So strong is the evidence that the site merely reflects the vicissitudes of the currency system in Britain that conclusions drawn from the coin evidence would be extremely misleading to historians of the period.

Whilst it is very easy to adumbrate general interpretative principles it is more difficult to establish ways in which the problems raised by gross external factors can be minimised in relation to the interpretation of individual sites. The first thing which must be established is what represents normality in the pattern of coinage of an archaeological province. This must be established for every period of time in which coins are present in large numbers. In practice this means a pattern for the Roman period and the medieval for western European sites, and for the Greek, Roman, Byzantine and Arab periods for sites in the Middle East. The establishment of regional patterns calls for a great deal of very detailed numismatic information and represents a formidable undertaking in terms of research, cataloguing and field-work. Every period will have its own pattern, as will each area, and extrapolation from one to another, even within a unified political system, can be dangerous and misleading. Figure 13 shows the spread of coinage found during the excavation of the Athenian Agora plotted on the same basis as the material from sites in Roman Britain.[8] It is clear that very similar general tendencies are present, but significant deviations from the north-west European pattern are discernible. For instance, the coinage of Carausius (period 20) is not found in the east because his political power was restricted to Britain and parts of Gaul; he is an irrelevance in an eastern coin list. By the same token, whereas the coinage of period 24 is very scarce in the west it is extremely prolific in the east. This coinage did not enter the west because Constantius II was anxious to keep his Caesar, Julian, as short of money as possible in order to prevent him having access to enough funds to raise a revolt. At the same time Constantius banned from circulation all coinage issued earlier than AD 354. These two decisions, both entirely political in origin, establish the characteristic feature of period 24 in Britain and Gaul. In the east no such considerations prevailed – there was no Magnentian coinage to banish and no potential revolt in the offing. As a result an abundance of coinage is found throughout the east at a period when it is virtually absent in the west. So how do we overcome

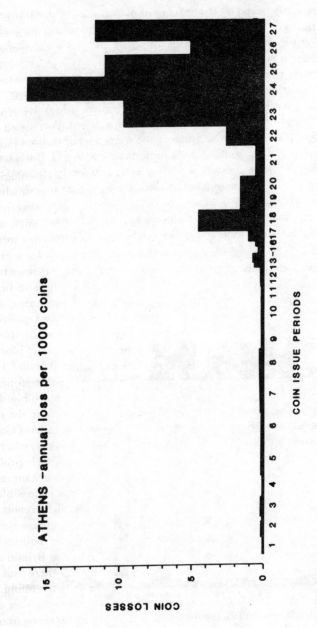

13. Athens coin losses.

the impediments raised by the absence of patterns for many areas and periods and, where they exist, how do we overcome the deadening effect on chronological deductions imposed by the weight of the pattern where it has been established?

If we revert to consideration of the graphs for British sites we can look for deviations from these patterns and hypothesise about the reasons for the deviation. The most obvious case to look for is one where the very high points of the histograms are absent. We cannot say with confidence that a site has undergone some sort of trauma in low coin deposit periods if coins of those periods are not found. But if there are no coins of a high deposit period we can confidently claim such a trauma; this really is a case where the absence of coins represents an occupational hiatus.

Figure 14 shows the coinage found in two contexts associated with the Roman fort of Vindolanda, Chesterholm, in Northumberland.

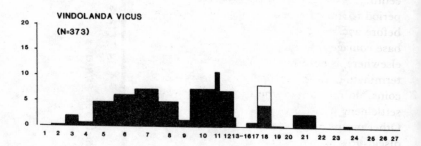

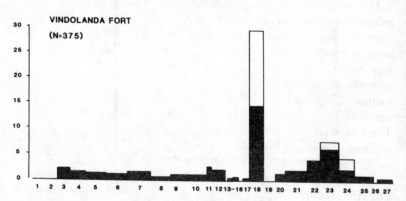

14. Vindolanda *vicus* and fort coin losses.

The fort was founded in the first century and continued to be garrisoned, through several phases of rebuilding, into the early years of the fifth century.[9] Although not as intensively excavated as the nearby fort at Corbridge, the coins from Vindolanda reflect, in a manner characteristic of military sites, the occupation attested by both epigraphic and documentary sources.

Outside the fort was an extensive civilian settlement which has been excavated to reveal a variety of elaborate stone buildings of two phases of construction.[10] A comparison between the coins found in the fort with those found in the vicus is instructive and shows how the overall coin picture of a site is in reality made up of individual numismatic incidents, the details of which may be lost in the wider contextual study. The analysis of the two contexts at Vindolanda shows that, whilst the fort was garrisoned for nearly four centuries, occupation of the civilian settlement ceased abruptly just after the middle of the third century. A closer examination of the coins shows that the few coins of period 19 from the vicus, which always dominates British sites, date to before 270 and that issues of the emperor Tetricus (270–73), whose base coinage makes up the bulk of the material plotted as period 19 elsewhere, is not found at Vindolanda. This argues for a very abrupt termination of the occupation. The coins, or rather the absence of coins, do not answer the question of where the civilians from the settlement went; they only disclose a piece of neutral information. Other means must be devised to answer the questions raised by such disclosures from the coin record.

Having looked at coins on the broad scale let us turn to study the micro-environment of coin finds. The examination of individual site clusters can yield significant results. A computerised study of the association of coins and pottery found during the excavation of the legionary fortress at Usk, in South Wales, brought to light an anomolous association of high value coins and specific pottery types on a single closed context.[11] The coins were silver *denarii* and the pottery consisted of the lids of amphorae, the standard storage jar for liquids. The Usk fortress dates from the reign of Nero (54–68) and the coins represent a considerable monetary loss for the period. It is a loss quite out of keeping with the sort of losses recorded elsewhere on the site both in terms of numbers of coins and the denominational structure. The circumstances of the loss might suggest that a high degree of coin activity was taking place in one small area and that this was one in which a large number of coin-based transactions took place. It suggests, too, that the area was one in which recovery of lost coins would be difficult or where fallen coins would be easily overlooked. One can imagine such an environment to be inside a building with poor lighting, with a floor which allowed dropped coins to be trampled in and where there was an intimate association between coins being used and amphorae, represented by the lids, being opened and the contents sold. But this context is within a legionary fortress and it is not usual to associate shops with the interior of military installations. Is there any corroborative evidence for commerce actually to have taken place on army property as opposed to outside the fortress gates? There is an instance of such evidence. In his description of the layout of the legionary fortress of the armies of the Republic, some two centuries before the foundation of Usk, the Greek historian Polybius describes just such a situation. Adjacent to the centre of the fortress was what he describes as the forum, an area in which merchants gathered to trade with the soldiers, to buy their loot and to provide them with home comforts to moderate the discomforts of the campaigning life. Usk was a fortress in the middle of barbarian territory when it was founded, at the very limits of the Empire. It is possible that in such a dangerous situation merchants, who in more peaceful circumstances would have been confined to trading outside the fortress, were allowed into the security of the fortification. Or, perhaps, the army itself set up a commercial operation, a sort of Neronian Naafi, for the benefit of the troops. An inscription from the fortress of Legio III Augusta, stationed at Lambeisis in Numidia, shows that two junior officers of the legion were in charge of the covered market situated outside the fortress, so that the association of the legionary forces with commerce is not unknown.[12] Presumably at least some of the things sold in the market were produced by the legion on the extensive landholdings which it would have been allocated, and on which, as we know from inscriptional evidence, livestock would have been reared or timber resources developed.

This is only one possible interpretation of the coin evidence but it is a speculation which opens up a new perspective on the activities of the Roman army. It also demonstrates the place which coin studies can play in evolving new ways of looking at excavations in association with literary evidence and other classes of material from the site. By comparing coin use on an area by area basis within the context of the single excavation we can develop on the individual site the technique we have advocated for comparison of site by site distributions on the macro-scale.

Whilst the establishment of the 'normal' distribution of coins is the desideratum and should always be attempted for major sites (that is, those with a lot of coin for the numismatist to work upon), most practising archaeologists require something less profound from their specialists and will want, in the first place, to answer the question 'how does it affect my dating?' Whilst histograms give a possible framework for viewing coin evidence overall, the value of the individual coin in its context is still of paramount interest. We have already seen that individual coins can have long lives, up to several centuries in some cases, and to this extent confining the study of coins to the display format of the histogram does some violence to the evidence. The very rigidity of the boundaries of the visual display is an illusion because it fails to show the way that coins of each defined period are present in the currency of any later period. We must face the problem of how to establish how long a coin might be in circulation before becoming incorporated in an archaeological context. The short answer is that it cannot be done with confidence.

Coins are residual not only in stratigraphical positions but in the currency pool as well. To complicate the matter further different denominations in a currency system may have longer circulatory lives than other denominations. This point can be highlighted from the British reformed decimal coinage system. This consists of new coins dating from 1971 to the present day, with two exceptions, if we exclude the recently introduced pound coin. A high proportion of the ten- and five-pence pieces in circulation are hangovers from the pre-decimal system where they were the shilling and two shilling pieces. Those are now revalued and they circulate alongside the new coinage, although they bear the old denomination names. A problem will arise some day from the longevity of these coins in the current reformed pool of coinage, from which specimens are dropping out to infiltrate into the depositional strata now being formed which will be the archaeological contexts of the future.

There are a number of approaches to this problem of longevity. Firstly, documentary sources can be examined for direct information; secondly, hoards can be examined in order to establish the range of coins available for incorporation in them up to the date of the closure of the individual hoard. A third approach is through the study of stratified coin groups in order to determine the volume of residual material in a succession of contexts. All of these approaches can be generally useful, in an inferential manner, but offer no absolute scale by which one can judge a coin's active life expectancy.

An important documentary source which illustrates the longevity of coins in circulation in a stable currency system is the record of the recoinage of the English hammered silver coinage in 1696 and its replacement by milled coins. In all, some £6,882,907 19s 7d worth of old money was called in for recoining. This consisted of coins stretching back to the reign of Edward VI (1547–53); very heavily represented was the coinage of Elizabeth (1558–1603) – dating from after her own recoinage of 1601. It is salutary to be reminded that the Civil War was financed with late medieval coinage and that Cromwell's troops were furnished from the pay of the sailors who fought the Spanish Armada. But then we can find coins used to pay the Roman garrison of Britain in the second century AD which probably originated in money issued to defeat Hannibal.

Periodic changes, such as the recoinage discussed above, form notable barriers to the continuation in use of old coins. But only if the currency involved is of precious metal, which can be remelted and recirculated in a new form, will the demonetised coinage disappear almost entirely. Valueless base metal coinages will be dumped or languish in the home to be gradually lost. The fact that they will cease to appear in hoards, though, is a good indication of the fact of them having no further currency function. Archaeologically a horizon of valueless coins may be created which, as we have seen, can be misinterpreted as a revival of coin use rather than a certain sign of coin disuse.

One or two series of coins are known to have been subject to rapid turnover and these are of particular value to the archaeologist. There is clear indication that late Saxon and early Norman coinage in England was very strictly controlled and that the type of the silver penny was changed regularly on Michaelmas Day.[13] This change took place at six yearly intervals from 973 to the middle of the reign of Edward the Confessor (1042–1066) and thereafter at three yearly intervals until the system broke down in the anarchy of the reign of Stephen (1135–54). Theoretically each new issue of pennies demonetised the preceding coins and hoard evidence seems to confirm that, by and large, this actually did happen. A coinage system such as this, operating on a constant recycling principle, can be used to establish a sequence of dates from losses sustained within a very narrow time band.

Resort to a study of wear characteristics must acknowledge that the history in circulation of individual coins varies very much. Some coins may, for instance, be immobilised in hoards for long periods and only resume a circulatory life late in the history of a currency in unworn condition. Sometimes we can look at the condition of coins in contexts which are dated securely by other than numismatic means. If a structure is dated by epigraphic or documentary means then the coinage associated with the earliest structural phase can be examined for wear and for association with other coins. Studies of such deposits on Hadrian's Wall show that a good deal of Flavian coinage was still in use in the 120s AD, whilst the coinage found on the Antonine Wall which was built in the years 140–142, and occupied for only about twenty years, is overwhelmingly that of Trajan.[14] The coins associated with the victims of the eruption of Vesuvius in AD 79 provide a glimpse of the coinage carried in daily use by the citizens of Pompeii and Herculaneum. Purses found with the victims cover a remarkably wide range, the silver spanning the second century BC to the reign of Vespasian, and the copper and brass coins ranging from the reign of Augustus through to the year of the eruption.[15] All of this evidence simply reinforces what common sense would predict; it does not allow one to construct an absolute standard of wear linked to a fixed time element which would allow the archaeologist to estimate the lag between the production of a coin and its incorporation in his deposits. Attempts to assign periods of years have been made, but these are mere guesses and should be given no evidential weight. Each numismatist will have his own idea of the age of a coin based upon his own wide experience of the series in question and the handling of thousands of specimens from a wide variety of contexts. Numismatics remains an art not a science.

The archaeologist uses coin evidence in a broader context than the single site when he attempts to survey whole areas through the medium of the coin find records. An example of this use of coins is the classic study of D.F. Allen of the distribution of finds of the coins of the Iron Age tribes of Britain.[16] Allen postulated that the distribution, which showed discrete blocks of coin in well-defined geographical zones, corresponds to the political boundaries of the individual tribes.

This work has achieved wide acceptance and marked a watershed in the understanding of the century and a half before the Roman conquest of Britain. Such a survey depends on the collection of scattered references to coin finds in scholarly sources, local collections, local histories and, since the advent of metal detectors, in newspapers. These sources offer accounts which may very well vary in accuracy from the entirely accurate to the entirely inaccurate. How can we be sure that the material is really properly recorded and that it represents a body of coinage which is of ancient deposition?

First the investigator must approach even coins lodged in museums with a wary scepticism if they are in any way unusual. For instance the Roman town of Caerwent has produced several thousand Roman coins. Included with the collection are a number of Byzantine pieces and these have sometimes been cited as evidence for a continuous contact between sub-Roman South Wales and the Mediterranean world. But close investigation shows that these coins were a donation to the museum, not a find from the Caerwent site, which were filed away with the finds from the Roman town where they acquired a false provenance by association.

Coins which may be exotic in one area, say in Britain, usually turn out to be coins which are very common somewhere else. Almost inevitably they are the sort of coins which are sold to tourists in Italy, North Africa or the Middle East. Once the buyer finds that his holiday souvenirs are of no commercial value, they are given to the local museum or handed on to the children to play with. This process has been going on since the days of the Crusaders and two massive boosts were given to the import of exotic ancient coins to Britain by the activities of the British armies in Palestine under Allenby in the First World War and under Montgomery in North Africa in the Second. These alien items can usually be detected by the experienced investigator either because they are exotic, like the frequently met with coins of Egypt issued in the Roman period which were of use only locally and which never played any part in the general currency of the empire, or because they do not conform to the distribution pattern of mints normally found in the area of study. A case of the latter can be illustrated from the Roman coinage found in Scotland.[17]

Roman contact with Scotland, after the withdrawal of forces in the 160s AD, when the Antonine Wall frontier was given up, was formally limited to two invasions, by Septimius Severus in the early third century and by Constantius Chlorus in the early fourth. However, a great number of Roman coins have been recorded as casual finds throughout Scotland and these have been seen as evidence of continued diplomatic or commercial contacts, unrecorded in the scanty literature of Roman Britain.

From the end of the third century it was the invariable practice of the mints which produced the Roman coinage to sign their work with an abbreviated mint signature. In this way individual coins could be, and still can be, assigned to their place of origin. The supply of coinage to Britain, as to any other area, was very closely regulated. Supplies of coinage were drawn by the administration from the mints nearest to the place where it was needed each year to pay the state's expenses. However, from time to time mints involved in supplying Britain opened or closed or raised or lowered their rates of output so that there was a constant change in the volume of coins from individual mints, change in the course of supply and, in consequence, a strong period by period pattern which is characteristic of finds from British sites.

Figures 15 and 16 show what happens when the coins recorded as being found in Scotland are plotted against a collection of coins indisputably lost in the fourth century in Britain. There is clearly a vast discrepancy between the mint distribution of the coins from Scotland and those excavated at Corbridge. The latter conform exactly to the supply pattern found throughout the Roman sites of Britain, coming from mints located nearest to the island. The majority of the coins from Scotland derive from mints at the very extremity of the empire furthest from Britain especially those of Constantinople, Nicaea and Alexandria. Why are the coins from Scotland so different? Why do most come from mints so far away and why do they not come from Britain, surely the nearest source of Roman coins, if they were the medium through which contact between the areas was, in some manner, maintained? The answer is that the coins from Scotland are modern imports brought back by travellers to the east. They are typical of the rubbish sold to tourists. The evidential value of the whole collection is so compromised that it would be rash to use coinage as a yardstick to measure contacts between Rome and Caledonia in the late Roman period.

A positive contribution to regional numismatic and archaeological studies has been made by the application of a mathematical technique called transect analysis to the distribution of finds of Iron Age coinage

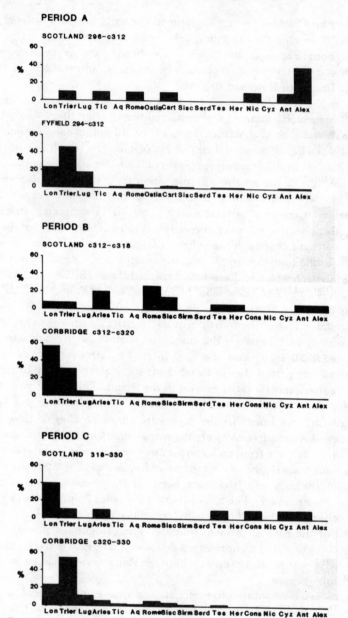

15. Fourth-century coins in Scotland 296–330.

PERIOD D

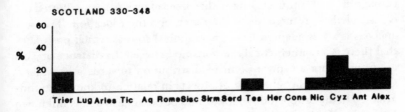

SCOTLAND 330-348

CORBRIDGE 330-348

PERIOD E

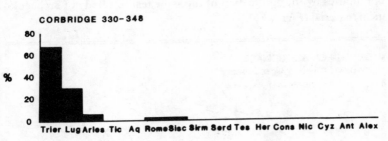

SCOTLAND 348-64

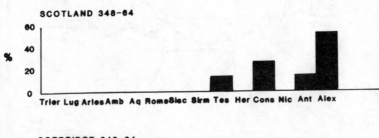

CORBRIDGE 348-64

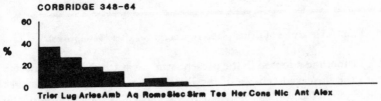

16. Fourth-century coins in Scotland 330–364.

in southern Britain.[18] This study is really an objective check on the subjective conclusions arrived at by Allen in his original study of tribal coinage in pre-Conquest Britain, discussed above. Allen attributed the coins to tribes on the basis of their style and their location. Transect analysis is a test adapted from geographical studies which postulates that there is a mathematical relationship between the distance objects are found from a central point of distribution towards a boundary. Observation of the behaviour of objects in relation to known boundaries led to the proposition that it would be possible to detect unknown boundaries by the application of the same test to a body of archaeological material (*Figure 17*).

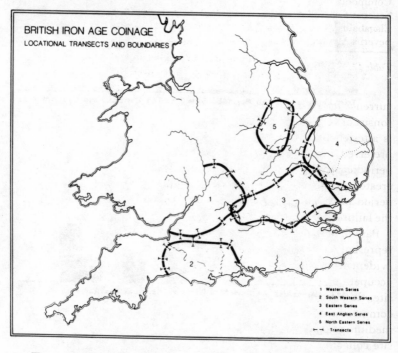

BRITISH IRON AGE COINAGE
LOCATIONAL TRANSECTS AND BOUNDARIES

1 Western Series
2 South Western Series
3 Eastern Series
4 East Anglian Series
5 North Eastern Series
Transects

17. Transect analyses of British Iron Age coinage (after Haselgrove).

The method adopted in the present study was to establish transects from the observed centres of the distribution of the tribal coinages which extended well across what was regarded as the location of the frontier between any two groups. The transects were normally about thirty miles long and, within each, all of the recorded coins in a ten mile width of territory was recorded. The mathematical manipulation of this data produced good results. The fall-off in the distribution coincided with the predicted pattern in many cases and, gratifyingly, these mathematical boundaries coincided with natural features like rivers and ranges of hills. A second factor, hitherto unsuspected, also emerged. This was the existence of 'frontier lands', zones between tribal groups which were apparently unoccupied but served as inter-tribal lands to separate contending peoples. Such zones are known to exist in the historical record, perhaps the best known being the scantily occupied border zone between England and Scotland. The phenom-enon is best seen in the present study in the east of England where a considerable gap exists between the boundaries of the coinage of the Iceni and the Coritani. Zones where coins of different groups interweave may indicate aggressive moves by one group into the territory of another or that the chronology of the coinage itself needs reinvestigation to establish whether what are currently regarded as contemporary issues are in fact successive coin series.

On the whole this analysis, though fraught with supposition and inference, does seem to derive new information from the coinage and opens up the possibility of detecting political boundaries between otherwise enigmatic peoples. An extension of this might be to apply the technique to investigate the extent of the territories controlled by the coin issuing cities of the Greco–Roman world or to establish the frontiers of Greek city states.

CHAPTER SEVEN

Coins and economic history

The usefulness of numismatic studies in the field of economic history varies with the alternative sources which are available. If there are ample documents, then avoid speculative studies based on coins; there is no virtue in turning away from actual economic records or from technical treatises where these exist. Nor should assumptions be made about coinage in undocumented periods without testing these assumptions on material from documented periods or without reference to the technical problems which are inherent in coin production wherever or whenever coins are manufactured. For example, if we are to estimate the productivity of a set of dies, the problems inherent in minting practices, which are known from documented accounts or have been elucidated by experiment, should be taken into account when constructing an economic model or postulating a hypothesis. If, for example, the physical examination of so-called 'coin moulds' of the Iron Age, the replication of metal pellets produced in them together with detailed observation of the physical characteristics of actual Iron Age coins, shows that the moulds could not have been used to produce the blanks on which coins were struck, it is no use at all to use the occurrence of moulds as an index of the economic or political status of the sites on which the moulds appear.[1] Nor can we erect elaborate spatial and hierarchical theories on them in the belief that moulds are direct evidence that the communities represented by the sites on which they are found had the resources and political independence to strike coinage.[2]

Attempts have been made to use mint records to establish correlations between coin survival in hoards and site finds and the volume of coinage originally produced. Such studies have not reached a point which would allow a precise relationship between output, survival and recovery. However, the pursuit of such studies may lay the basis on which a generalised theoretical view of coin behaviour may be established. In the meantime, experience of numismatic problems tends to suggest that specific coin regimes have their own specific behavioural traits, though these tend to be dictated by similar economic trends such as inflation, debasement, reforms, consumer preference and the availability of metals for conversion into coin.

Where no records whatsoever have survived, the study of the surviving coins themselves is the foundation of research and, because coins are a form of money, it might be expected that a study of coinage in the mass would yield unambiguous economic information. Unfortunately, as in so many branches of historical research, the data are, themselves, ambiguous. Factors can obtrude which compromise the value of the enquiry. Those factors may include an unequal survival or recovery of coins, changes in the currency studied which resulted in systematic withdrawal, or a collapse and devaluation which might result in an over-representation of specific valueless issues or denominations. Even if we duly take into account these kinds of factors we also need to take into account the fact that coins are not the only medium through which wealth can be stored, exchanges effected or payments made. Irrespective of the place of barter in an economy, the transfer of obligations through the medium of bills of exchange or less sophisticated credit arrangements may have a substantial impact on the volume of coinage produced and the denominations in use. We also know that the sort of coinage which is lost and subsequently recovered may well be quite unrepresentative of the sort of coinage used in commercial transactions. We cannot very accurately judge the wealth of a society, the volume of its trade and the true nature of its economic activity from small change when common sense tells us that really important deals were conducted through some other coin medium.

These considerations tend to limit enquiry to societies in which high denomination coins make up the bulk of the study material, and to press the researcher to concentrate on the evidence of hoards. If we are dealing with a society which produced a coinage of a simple denominational pattern, say only gold or silver coins, or one which relied heavily on a single denomination, a position occupied by the Roman *denarius* for several centuries, we might expect to be able to gain some insight into economic activity through observing the variations in the volume of coinage produced from time to time and through fluctuations in the intrinsic value of the individual coins.

How is such an investigation conducted? There are a number of stages, each of which has its speculative element. Firstly, a base must be established of clearly identified coin issues which have been studied to a point at which individual dies can be identified. Next a method of establishing the size of the issue must be sought. This is done by calculating the number of dies employed in the production of the coinage and attempting to establish, by practical experiment or other means, the number of coins produced from the calculated body of dies. Attaching the resulting statistics to a historical or economic framework may call for the deployment of archaeological or other evidence, or the resulting statistics may stand in isolation pointing by their very existence to a problem in an otherwise unexplored area of research.

A study of hoard evidence is the best way in which to establish a data base, since hoards yield a pattern of the relative frequency of individual issues within a coinage and, whilst those frequencies may be explicable in other than immediately economic terms by the need to give gifts, pay mercenaries, fund armies or defray the costs of buildings, these activities are themselves embedded in an economic matrix. Put simply, the marshalling of resources for any of these activities is the manifestation of the operation of an economic system, and the diffusion of wealth down the social pyramid, just as its accumulation for redistribution from the top of it, will have had widespread effects.

Study of a succession of hoards can be used to establish the relative size of individual issues, but quantitative studies require the estimation of the volume of each issue in order to gain some insight into the totality of the currency which may have been issued. Lacking records, numismatists have recourse to estimates based on practical experimentation, which can establish the mechanical limits on the speed of use and the life span of dies under the stress of production. They have also evolved statistical formulae from which can be calculated the number of dies available to produce a given series of coins.

Firstly, there is the problem of the number of dies. It is clearly impossible to compare what may be a total of many thousands of coins in order to establish by direct visual comparison how many dies were used in the production in a very large coinage. Consequently a sampling strategy must be adopted. Here the laws of probability theory come to the aid of the numismatist. If a coin is tossed in the air there is a fifty-fifty chance that it will land head-side up, and in an infinite series of throws there would be as many heads-up as tails-up throws. In a less than infinite series of throws the ratio of heads to tails will vary with chance, but the larger the number of throws the nearer to a fifty-fifty split will be the overall result. Mathematically, in 1000 throws the head, say, will appear on between 470 and 530 occasions, and on a related scale to infinity. Because of this constant we can, conversely, work out the number of throws which will have resulted in an observed frequency of incidents of heads if only the latter fact is recorded. This probability calculation can be extended to study a coinage in which a statistically significant sample of dies can be observed.

The method used for calculating the number of dies used in an observed coinage was evolved by C.S.S. Lyon and is known for convenience as the Lyon Formula:[3] $K = \frac{1}{m}(1 - e^{-m})$, where $K = \frac{z}{y}$ $m = \frac{y}{x}$. This formidable equation breaks down into the following components:

z = The number of dies (obverse) observed to be used in the hoard or coinage sample.
y = The total number of coins in the hoard or coinage sample.
e = The natural logarith base 2.71828.
x = The total number of dies used in the coinage as a whole.

The equation must, therefore, be solved for x but this cannot be done directly. However, it has been established that $\frac{y}{x}$ is a function of K which can be plotted graphically or, more easily, established by consulting a table of constants for this value, in relation to a series of likely coin problems, derived by Lyon.

To take an example from the published literature, suppose that 143 coins show 102 different obverse dies,[4] so that z = 102 and y = 143 and K = 0.173. The value for this function in the table is 0.72. Since m = 0.72 and y = 143, then 143/x = 0.72, and x = 143/0.72 = 199. So that our coins are derived from a population of about 200 obverse dies. Assuming a striking rate of 20,000–30,000 coins per die we may postulate that the 143 coins are representative of an original issue in the region of between 3,980,000 and 5,970,000 coins, giving a survival rate of between 1:27832 and 1:41748 specimens. This calculation depends on the assumption that all dies struck the same number of coins, an assumption which is, perhaps, unrealistic. However, checks made by calculating the die figures using this formula with actual known die numbers shows a very close agreement between the real figure and the theoretically derived one.

An advance on the consultation of a table of values of constants is the use of a computerised formula. The following programme can be run on any home- or micro-computer and is provided by D. Sellwood as a result of his work on Parthian coinage:

READY

```
10 REM DIE TOTAL PROGRAM
20 PRINT "TYPE IN NUMBERS OF COINS AND DIES REPRESENTED"
30 INPUT Y, Z
40 PRINT Y; Z
50 LET K = Z/Y
60 LET M = 1
70 LET Q = 1 - EXP( - M)
80 LET N = Q/K
90 IF ABS < (M - N)/M) < .001 THEN 120
100 LET M = N
110 GOTO 70
120 LET X = Y/M
130 PRINT
140 PRINT "MOST PROBABLE TOTAL NUMBER OF DIES IS";
150 IF X - INT (X) < .5 THEN 180
160 PRINT INT (X) + 1
170 GOTO 190
180 PRINT INT(X)
190 END
```

READY

TYPE IN NUMBERS OF COINS AND DIES REPRESENTED 45, 30

MOST PROBABLE TOTAL NUMBER OF DIES IS 51

The next process is to find some method by which the estimated die figures can be related to actual production figures. Here two approaches have been tried, one based on experimentation, the other on documentary evidence. The latter approach has been employed by M. Crawford in his work on the coinage and finances of the Roman Republic.[5] Crawford's study is based upon the observation of the number of obverse dies used to produce the state's successive issues of silver coinage. As we have noted, obverse dies are more carefully used than reverse dies, so fewer are produced.

The productive capacity of the Republican die series is based on an invaluable piece of literary evidence. In 82 BC the proconsul C. Annius was sent with an army of two legions to fight against Q. Sertorius in Spain. Here he campaigned for about a year. The money needed to pay Annius' army would have amounted to about 3,000,000 *denarii* and it seems that a special issue was produced to meet this need. The number of obverse dies known to have been involved in the production amount to 130. Allowing for under-use and breakages this suggests that about 30,000 coins were produced from each die. On the basis of this figure we can estimate some of the sums used to finance the armies of the contending factions in the Civil Wars which brought about the end of the Republic. For instance the coinage of Mark Antony struck shortly before the Battle of Actium in 31 BC, which brought Octavian to power and initiated the imperial era of Roman history, was struck from 864 obverse dies in the name of 23 legions.

On the basis of 30,000 coins per die this issue should have amounted to 25,920,000 (= 26,000,000) *denarii*. At the time the cost of a legion stood at three million *denarii* a year so that a full year's cost of Antony's army would have been 23 × 3,000,000 *denarii* (= 69,000,000 *denarii*). On the figures calculated from the die study it looks as if the army received its regular pay just before the final action, since they were paid thrice annually, and the rounded up production estimate is very close to the 23,000,000 *denarii* which would have been the sum needed to pay the regular four monthly *stipendium*.

Such calculations inspire confidence in the general methodology of combining die studies with literary evidence in the Roman period. A further aspect of Crawford's study is that, by deducting the annual costs of military pay, which varied from time to time, it is possible to get some glimpse of expenditure above and beyond simple military needs and to strike some sort of balance sheet for the cost of the expansion of Roman power in the Mediterranean and the creation of a world capital in Rome itself.

However, there is no certainty that Roman production figures have validity elsewhere. It may be noted that, whilst medieval documentary evidence suggests that totals in the region of 30,000 coins were achieved, it also suggests that production could be as low as 8,500 coins per die. Clearly the production figures are influenced by the availability of bullion to coin rather than the mechanical properties of the dies themselves. This leads inevitably to a consideration of whether experimental methods alone, which give a mechanical maximum, are reliable when they are unsupported by other evidence. At best we can establish a physical limit on the size of a coinage even if in reality the real limit was one imposed by economic or political considerations.

The production of Greek silver tetradrachms has been studied in a completely practical manner by examining all extant Greek bronze dies and replicating them in metallic composition and design.[6] Coins were then struck from the dies until the end of their useful life, using silver of the same type as was used in antiquity. This experiment showed that about 8000 coins could be produced before the reverse die became unusable. This die fractured at the end on which the hammer blow fell and eventually became too short to handle, but the face of the die was not seriously compromised by use by this stage of production. On the other hand the same experiment showed that an obverse die could produce between 10,000 and 16,000 coins before showing unacceptable signs of wear. These figures were derived from striking heated blanks; the figures for cold struck coins is significantly lower – 4000 from the upper and 8000 from the lower die. Clearly the extrapolation of these results to actual numismatic studies would require the establishment of whether a coinage understudy had been hot or cold struck, something which can in fact be ascertained by the microscopic examination of the inferior composition of a specimen of the coinage under review.

It may be worth observing at this stage that these practical experiments coincide very closely with results obtained by a study of the only detailed minting figures which have survived from the ancient world.[7]

Within the sanctuary of Delphi, various Greek city states had established guardianship of individual shrines, with the Amphictions, a wide confederation of cities, controlling the important shrine of

Pythian Apollo. This shrine was wrecked by an earthquake in 373–2 BC and funds were raised from a levy on the towns of the Amphictionic League and from voluntary subscriptions from other communities. Work was interrupted by the Third Sacred War and Delphi was sacked and occupied by the Phokians between 355 and 346 BC. During their occupation the Phokians melted down 10,000 talents worth of liturgical vessels, offerings and deposited treasures in order to pay their mercenary army.

The Phokians were defeated, their city razed to the ground and an indemnity imposed upon them to repay the sequestrated 10,000 talents. This sum was to be paid in instalments and these instalments were recorded by the Amphictions at Delphi as part of an elaborate series of inscriptions which add up to an account of the budget for the rebuilding of the temple of Apollo. The accounts are very detailed and record the volume of coinage of various origins which was melted down and restruck as Amphiptionic League coin to pay for the building operations. The coinage was struck between 336 and 334 BC, the value of coinage being between 125 and 175 talents (there is an ambiguity in the inscription on this point) in three denominations.

From the surviving coins, statistical probability indicates that the Amphiptionic staters were struck from not less than seven and not more than nine obverse dies, and it seems likely that at least 80 per cent of the coin struck was in this denomination. On the basis of 125 talents this would amount to 210,000 staters, and on the basis of 175 talents 330,750 staters. Taking the minimum figure of production and the highest estimate of dies we get a figure of $\frac{210,000 \text{ coins}}{9 \text{ dies}} = 23,333$ coins per die. This figure is higher than the figure experimentally determined, but the dies in the Amphictionic coinage were used to their utmost limits, as the worn look of uncirculated coins attests. This estimate and the experimental work suggests that Greek coinage could be produced in a very much greater volume than had been hitherto suspected.

Controversial use has been made of the combined factors of die estimation and experimental die output.[8] An attempt to determine the output of the coinage of Offa of Mercia, based on a similar but less mathematically sound formula than that of Lyon, provoked lively controversy and led to acrimonious dispute between protagonists in the fray. As a result of such episodes economic historians have looked upon the effort of numismatists to provide statistics where none survives with considerable suspicion. None the less, as we have seen in the case of the Roman Republic, speculative quantification can be undertaken and illuminating results obtained.

An examination of the coinage of the imperial period leads to some interesting conclusions which appear to be at variance with the Republican study and underline some of the hazards in the numerical approach. An extremely close study of the coinage of the reign of Domitian (81–96) indicates that, on the best estimate possible from a combination of statistical and probability calculations based on observations of die links within a large number of hoards, on site finds and collections, the annual output of *denarii* during the reign fluctuated very considerably.[9] Figure 18 shows the calculated annual output of *denarii* plotted against the only base statistic which can be calculated with reasonable confidence – the annual cost of military pay. Domitian raised pay to 300 *denarii* a year for legionaries in the early 80s and this calculation is based on the new rate. An overall figure of 150 *denarii* a year is assigned to auxiliaries to allow for the wide variation of pay between different sorts of units, and the calculation assumes an army of twenty-eight legions with an equal number of auxiliaries. The base figure for annual pay calculated on the propositions outlined above is 69.3 million *denarii* a year. When the estimated production figures are expressed against this datum the shortfall is enormous and varies from 36,905,000 *denarii* in 92, when production was at a maximum to a 'deficit' of 67,945,500 *denarii* in AD 84. What conclusions can be drawn from these apparently vast discrepancies?

We should be aware of a number of factors. Firstly, the army pay figure is an estimate, though it is one which is unlikely to be very far from a reasonable approximation of the true sum. Secondly, we should closely examine the assumptions on which the calculation of the annual output is based. We assume a production figure of 30,000 coins per die and the number of dies are an estimate of a probability. In the last analysis the estimate depends on the survival of coins to form a data base for the probability estimate. If for any reason coins do not survive they cannot add their weight to any ensuing calculations. Domitian's coinage has an inherent problem in just this area and at just the period when the calculated production/outgoings deficit is most pronounced. In 82 Domitian raised the standard of the *denarius* from a mean silver content of 90 per cent to an enhanced one of 98 per cent. This high standard was maintained until AD 85 when the silver content

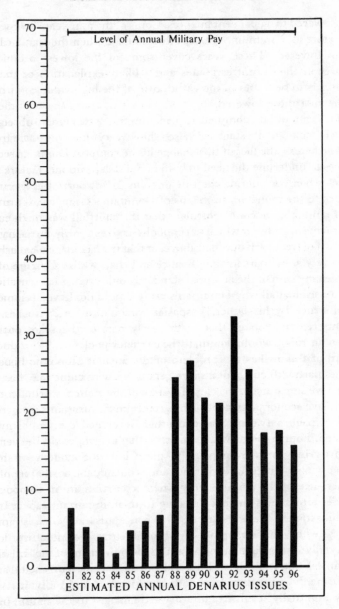

18. Domitianic denarius production and military outlay.

was lowered to 93 per cent fineness. Coins of the four years 82–85 were therefore at a premium against other coinage when the standard was again lowered. These years cover some of the lowest production figures in the output estimates and a likely explanation of the low figures is to be found in the withdrawal of the high value coins when the standard was lowered.

This cannot be a complete explanation, since two years subsequent to the change of standard also show very low output figures. Nevertheless, the fact of this change in the status of Domitian's coins serves to underline the need to hold in mind depositional factors at all times when considering the role of coins in any sort of enquiry. To return to the monetary problems of Domitain's reign, as exemplified by Figure 18, we could postulate that the shortfall was made up by payments in gold, for which not enough survives to provide the basis of the sort of treatment outlined above, or that fresh coinage played only a relatively small part in state finance and that, whilst a currency was stable, any coin of the accepted standard could pass as current. There is no reason at all why Domitian's army should not have been paid in coin struck by his father, Vespasian, or his brother, Titus. In any event, reason 'ictates that in the early part of the reign coins of previous rulers would dominate the currency pool.

All of this makes the problem of the ancient economic historian particularly difficult, but a more general view of coins may be taken when we step outside the closed system of the Roman world. In an all pervasive economic system such as the Roman, variations in currency and coinage between areas and other developed economies hardly existed. Fourth-century laws do attest that a profit could be made by transferring coins from place to place but this evidence is in an exceptional political circumstance and is outside the normal economic experience of the empire. Only when economies are in competition for resources does currency dealing form an important aspect of the mobilisation of these resources. This concept is one which is familiar today when the strengths of national currencies fluctuate quite markedly; these fluctuations result in the movement of money, in the technical financial sense, into and out of specific currencies. Such movements are initiated by both governments and individuals and may eventually result in quite marked changes in the nature of the currencies involved in the transactions. Weak currencies will lose value and may need to be revalued and such revaluation will probably call for the issue of new types of coins. The operation of such monetary factors may be detectable if we know how to look for them. In looking for them there are two aspects to be borne in mind – the currency affecting and that affected.

The best illustration of this applied to numismatic research is Grierson's study of the coinage system of western Europe, the Arab states and the Byzantine empire in the last decade of the seventh and first decade of the eighth century.[10] The study set out to examine three coincidental phenomena: the abandonment of silver coinage by the Byzantine state, the introduction of a uniform silver currency by the Arab caliphate and the change in the Frankish and Anglo-Saxon kingdoms of Europe from a gold coinage derived from that of Rome to a silver coinage based on a Germanic metrological system.

After the conquest of the Sassanian empire and the Roman provinces of Africa, Egypt, Palestine and Syria the monetary policy of the new Moslem administration was to leave intact the coinage system which it had inherited. In the formerly Roman areas, de-Christianised copies of the gold *solidus* and the copper *follis* were produced, and in Persia the Sassanian silver coinage, with the addition of the name of the Arab governor of the province, continued to appear. In the Byzantine empire a large-scale silver coinage appeared during the reign of Heraclius (610–641) with the silver *hexagram*, weighing *c.*6.5 gr., being tariffed at twelve to the 4.55 gr. *solidus*. In Europe the Franks and Anglo-Saxons produced gold tremisses (one-third *solidi*). In the east Roman world the relative value of gold to silver, by weight, was 1:18, and in barbarian Europe the ratio was 1:12 but with no silver circulating so that the exchange ratio was rather notional.

In the last decade of the seventh century and first decade of the eighth, the caliph Abd al-Malik initiated a comprehensive reform of the coinage of the Arab world. Abandoning the traditional Roman gold coin standard, he issued gold dinars on a 4.25 gr. weight standard, and silver dirhems weighing 2.97 gr. In this system gold played a very small role and virtually the entire weight of the coinage for taxation and private transactions was borne by the silver currency. The gold dinar was valued at twenty dirhems, giving a gold to silver ratio of 1:14. Thus, in the early eighth century three gold/silver ratios existed: the Frankish 1:12, the Byzantine 1:18 and the newly established Arab 1:14 ratio. In this situation, and given that the predilection of the Arab authorities was to establish a uniform inter-provincial silver coinage system where none had previously existed, the caliphate was in a unique position to undertake a manipulation of what would now be called the foreign exchange market. Byzantium wanted gold, which it valued higher than silver in relation to the Arab world. The Arab world wanted silver, which it valued higher than gold in relation to its neighbour. In consequence, gold drained rapidly out of the Arab world and silver out of the Byzantine. Exactly at the time of the reform of Abd Al-Malik the huge output of Byzantine hexagrams ceased. In Europe a different situation prevailed. Here gold was valued at a lower ratio to silver than in either the Arab or the Byzantine world, to the extent that an Arab withdrawal of gold in exchange for silver could be turned to a profit by passing cheap gold on to the Byzantine state in exchange for silver at their exchange ratio. As a result, gold drained out of Europe and the silver denier took over as the unit of currency in place of the gold *tremissis*.

This sort of analysis depends, ultimately, on an appreciation of weight standards and the establishment of a firm chronological framework for the emission of specific denominations or coin types. On a very broad scale we can detect similar world systems in operation at other periods. The expansion of Portuguese power through the control of gold from the Gambia, which came with the exploration of the African continent, is paralleled by that of Spain with the exploitation of Mexican silver after her penetration of South America in the sixteenth century. Such influxes of wealth are not an unmixed economic blessing and if we are to extrapolate from documented periods to undocumented ones, we should note that historically the unrestricted growth of money or coin circulation in these circumstances seems to lead to inflation and a rise in production costs.

The corrolary of an abundance of high value coinage may not be a widespread blessing and the equation of coinage with wealth is probably too simple. The control of a silver supply at Laurion no doubt led to high prices in fifth-century Athens, and though much of this wealth was spent in public works projects, such as the rebuilding of the Acropolis, we can be sure that the apparent wealth of Athens in its heyday, as evidenced by its abundant surviving coins, is illusory as far as the majority of the population, who would have had to contend with price inflation, was concerned. To counter such an economic cycle, which must result in domestic industry outpricing itself, governments may resort to deliberate debasement of their own currency, as did the Spanish in the sixteenth century, in order to make it less attractive to other parties and curtail its outflow from the domestic economy. That the level of monetary control reached such sophisticated levels before modern monetarist theory was expounded can be seen in the Ptolemaic economy of Egypt, where a coinage significantly baser than that of the rest of the Mediterranean was issued for domestic use and was the required medium of exchange for transactions of other states wishing to gain access to the enormous range of commodities available from Egypt. This policy ensured a steady flow of good silver into Egypt in exchange for the Ptolemaic coin needed in payment for goods and services within Egypt itself by overseas traders.

CHAPTER EIGHT

Scientific aspects of coin studies

The amount of information which can be extracted from the visual inspection of a coin is limited. We can read, if they be vouchsafed, the titles of the issuing authority or ruler; sometimes the date of the striking of the coin can be seen and frequently some trite motto will adorn a conventionalised figure or scene on the reverse. A few further details may be included in the design such as the denomination, though this is rare before the late medieval period, and perhaps some indication of which mint produced the coin. In cases where a severe change in the metal used in production has taken place, one can detect which coins of an issue are of poorer metal and which better. But there are further stages in the investigation of coinage which can yield an amazing amount of information and which demand the use of scientific techniques. In the past few decades a new field of research has been developed between scientists and numismatists.

What sorts of problems have been investigated? Primarily the research has been devoted to the study of coinage standards and metallurgy, with special emphasis on the composition of coins and the sources of the metals incorporated in their fabric. But other aspects are under investigation, such as the residual magnetic properties of coin metals which may allow coins of the same type to be assigned to different mint centres, each mint having a different magnetic 'signature'.[1] The analytical techniques used in research can be broadly divided into two categories – destructive and non-destructive.

Destructive analysis

On the whole the owners of coins, whether they be individual collectors or the curators of public collections, are reluctant to submit coins to destructive analytical processes since the gain in knowledge which results is bought at the price of the loss of part or whole of the coin investigated. However, there are some series of coins in which there are enough extant specimens for some sacrifices to be made in the cause of science. For instance, some Roman or Hellenistic issues still survive in thousands of specimens, as do certain medieval coins, notably those from the last two centuries of the Byzantine empire. Even so there is a reluctance to use destructive methods because they are so time-consuming and the essence of the scientific study of coins is to achieve as many experimental results as possible. Since time is money, the investigation of money must be economical of time.

The classic destructive method of analysis is by wet-chemistry.[2] A sample of the coin is dissolved in nitric acid and the resulting precipitate is analysed by individual tests designed to localise the constituent elements present in the sample and to establish, within very fine limits, the proportions in which they are present. Preparation of the sample is, of course, critical and care is taken that superficial corrosion products which are not intrinsic to the original composition are excluded. This means that the preparation of the sample calls for heroic surgery. In order to ascertain that corrosion products have not penetrated the specimen to a point which would invalidate its use in analysis, the coin is broken in two so as to obtain a granular break through its core. If the core reveals no deep corrosion, all surface deposits are removed by filing the faces of the coin. This drastic preparation is necessary because there is a tendency in alloys for elements of the mix to migrate. In a copper/silver alloy, for instance, copper near the surface of the coin leaches out leaving a richer silver deposit. This process is known as 'surface enrichment' and is one which would inevitably change the proportions of metals, within detectable limits in a wet analysis, were it not to be corrected by removing the affected layers of the specimen. Unfortunately, some coins, such as the base Roman silver of the mid-third century, were deliberately surface enriched to enhance their appearance. Inevitably in this case drastic preliminary treatment can distort the analytic results achieved.

A number of analyses have been published which have established, to minute standards of accuracy, the metallurgical content of a selection of Roman coinage in all metals ranging in date from the

Republic to the late fourth century. These results are not themselves of sufficient number to answer all of the problems which are outstanding in our knowledge of the evolution of this currency and the changes in standard which it underwent. However, pinpointing changes in composition augments our other sources for the political history of the empire, especially from the mid-second century to the mid-fourth, when documentary sources are extremely poor.

Knowing that political crises were very frequently accompanied by debasements of the currency it is possible to establish a firmer chronology of these events by detecting changes in the composition of the coins themselves. Sufficient full analyses now exist to use their results to check on the accuracy of less complete methods of analysis, such as micro-chemical analysis, or non-destructive particle based methods.

Wet-chemical analysis is capable of detecting minute components of material within the structure of a coin. There are more than 130 elements, but of these only fifteen are found in influential proportions in coinage and of these six are normally sought in analysis: silver, copper, lead, tin, zinc and lead. Trace elements of nickel, cobalt, bismuth and iron can be important in determining the source of the metal used in the coinage and may be very important in determining whether apparently similar coins are struck at one or more mint. Useful results can be obtained from less protracted wet analyses if the questions asked of the process are carefully framed; normally the problem under review will revolve round the proportion of silver present in relation to base metal.

An example of the results which can be obtained in a problem oriented analysis can be illustrated from a hoard of coins found in the civil settlement of the fort at Piercebridge, Co. Durham.[3] This was a straightforward collection of coins of the sort hoarded as a hedge against the debasement of the currency which took place during the Gallic Empire (258–73). The hoard consisted of 130 coins of which all but two fell into the years 235 to 262. The majority were issues of Postumus whose coinage was debased in a series of steps from a high of c.20 per cent to a low of c.4.5 per cent silver.

The hoard represented a consistent group of issues terminating with three virtually unworn coins of 262. However, a further element was present in two coins which had been ascribed to 268 by the standard, authoritative work on this coin series. Why the six year gap? How could a hoard remain intact to be added to in this manner? Could the date of these coins be wrong? Since the coinage of Postumus is debased in a discrete series of falling standards an analysis might disclose whether these coins fell into the last stage of debasement, which they should on the dating ascribed to them, or into an earlier stage of the currency. Chemical analysis showed that the silver content was very high, over 20 per cent, which placed the issue early in the reign of Postumus rather than at the end – a conclusion subsequently confirmed by further hoard evidence.

On the whole destructive analytical methods have been eschewed for the reasons outlined above, the difficulty of obtaining material for examination and the time taken by the process, a factor which makes it extremely expensive. Consequently a search has taken place for a method, or methods, by which analytical results can be achieved which do not harm the specimen, can be rapidly deployed so that a large body of material can be examined and is not ruinously expensive. A number of techniques have been developed, not in the field of chemistry but in that of physics. These techniques are widely used in the examination of metal artefacts elsewhere in archaeology but the special problems which arise in the investigation of coinage call for a full appreciation of the methods, their advantages and shortcomings, before the numismatist or archaeologist attempts to initiate a programme of research in which the techniques are employed.[4]

Non-destructive analysis

X-Ray Fluorescence Analysis

The operation involved in this process is to focus an X-ray beam at the coin in order to excite the elements represented in its composition in such a manner that a stream of secondary X-rays is emitted, proportional to the elements present. The secondary X-rays are focused through a crystal and the spectrum of light thus created is analysed by a spectrometer. Since each element occupies a different place within the spectrum, and the value of the element registers proportionally in the width of space which it occupies in the spectrum, a quantitative correlation can be established for the components in the object analysed by comparison with prepared standards covering a range of alloys and mixtures of elements. Measuring the spectrum widths, once done by manual means from a photographic strip, is done by a gas-filled proportional counter coupled to a graphing machine.

The problem with this process is that the secondary X-rays are generated at a depth of only 30–100 microns below the surface (1 micron = 1/1000 mm), so that the effect of surface enrichment, discussed above, looms very large. However, the modern milliprobe XRF apparatus operates over a very small area and the initiatory X-ray beam covers no more than 1 mm of the surface. This small area can be cleaned without harming the appearance of a coin or diminishing its value. The area must be prepared by removing, by abrasion, all superficial deposits as well as the surface enriched layer. To establish that a layer unaffected by surface enrichment has been reached the coin is 'read' and cleaned until consecutive readings give the same values.

In reality a number of points on the surface or edge of the coin must be examined because the homogeneity of even very pure coins is not complete, and, at the microscopic scale of investigation, it is possible to read from a single high or low value grain of material within the coin matrix. XRF cannot be used on coins which are known to be inhomogenous of structure. The Roman base silver coinage of the third century, for instance, contains discrete lumps of copper and silver and there is no method of ensuring that the probe will be dealing with a representative part of the whole coin alloy.

XRF has been used with very great success in analysing large series of coins in order to establish their chronology through the decline of their precious metal content. Largest of these series of analyses is that which has been undertaken of the imperial *denarius* from the reign of Augustus to its effective demise in the reign of Gordian III (238–44). This considerable achievement has opened up an important period of Roman monetary and political history to quantitative investigation by economic historians for the first time.[5]

Similar to XRF is Proton Induced X-ray Emission, in which protons (actively charged particles) are used to irradiate the sample. PIXE has a greater penetrative ability than XRF, so the secondary X-rays are produced further into the matrix of the coin. Moreover, the proton beam can be aimed with great accuracy at a spot even smaller than is possible with XRF, and consequently the preparation of an even smaller area of the coin surface is necessary.

Neutron Activation Analysis (NAA)

NAA is the most important of the non-destructive procedures available to the coin analyst because, unlike XRF, or its derivatives, the whole body of the coin is included in the investigation. The subject is bombarded with neutrons from an atomic source which excites the nuclei of the elements of the coin. Some of these nuclei are converted, under this treatment, into unstable radioactive isotopes. In turn these unstable isotopes decay to form stable isotopes and, in doing so, give off radiation. The strength of the gamma rays produced by this chain of events is relative to the amount of the element producing the reaction. Different elements produce distinctive and identifiable gamma radiations.

One considerable drawback of neutron activation analysis is that inaccuracy can arise from the shielding effect created by the thickness of metal in heavy coins. A further problem is that the method cannot determine the lead content of a coin since this element is impervious to radiation to the extent that it does not form unstable isotopes.

Because NAA treats the whole coin, rather than the surface levels, it is particularly suitable for the investigation of coins with an in-homogenous structure. A full investigation, in which everything down to trace elements is analysed, calls for an irradiation in an atomic reactor. However, less complete analysis can be achieved using a less powerful neutron source, and the normal problem of defining silver content can be accomplished by submitting the specimen to a low intensity beam of neutrons produced from a modest radioactive source. Current experimental procedures can process a coin in less than three minutes and leave the specimen available for immediate display or return to its owner.

The methodology of the low irradiation process, as developed by A.A. Gordus of the University of Michigan, illustrates the relative simplicity of the process.[6] The coin and a silver blank, or coin of known silver composition, are introduced to the neutron source for one minute. The radio-activity count of the two objects is then determined separately but simultaneously by radiation counters. Because silver absorbs neutrons, the numbers reaching through the full thickness of the coin vary with the thickness of the coin and the amount of silver present. To eliminate the effects of this factor the radiation present in the silver blank is taken into consideration, since this radiation is relative to the number of neutrons that have passed through the coin into the disc. The more silver in the coin, or the thicker the coin, the less radioactive effect will be experienced by the blank disc. A fixed value for the penetrative effect of neutrons through coins of various thicknesses and known composition has been established experimentally, and a constant (R) established which allows for the effect of coin thickness on the ultimate estimation of silver content to be overcome.

$$\frac{\text{Radiation from coin}}{\text{Radiation from disc} \times \text{weight of coin} \times \text{average R}} = \frac{\text{Percentage silver}}{\text{in coin}}$$

It is worth noting that very thin coins are not susceptible to this treatment because the factors governing the establishment of the value of R break down.

All of these methods of examination call for the coin to travel to the laboratory or reactor. Understandably the curators of public collections are reluctant, or unable, to release material to researchers and attempts have been made to avoid the necessity of bringing the coin to the apparatus. A particular problem applies where coins are in collections in countries without any sort of research facilities.

An interesting approach to the problem is the development of the 'coin-streak' technique. The edge of the coin is cleaned over a small area to eliminate the surface enriched layer, then gently rubbed on a roughened quartz tubing. Less than 0.001 gr. of coin metal is removed for subsequent analysis by NAA. The brightened area from which the sample has been removed on the edge of the coin quickly discolours to the overall tone of the rest of the coin. This method allows the worker to collect material for later examination from public collections and other sources, rather as a normal researcher collections bibliographic references for later evaluation. Unfortunately there is no certainty that the streak will be representative of the coin as a whole and all of the objections to the validity of the results experienced with other surface biased investigations must be raised when evaluating published results achieved by this method.[7]

An extension of the methods of investigation dependent on radioactive reactions is the alliance of elements of wet-chemistry to mass spectrographic techniques. To overcome the effects of surface enrichment, and to protect the surface appearance of the coin, a method of taking a horizontal sample out of the body of the soin has been developed using extremely fine drills. This technique has the further advantage of securing a cross section of the body of the coin so that problems of inhomogeneity are largely overcome. Once it is obtained the drilling may be investigated directly by NAA or chemically precipitated and investigated by either the PIXE or the XRF procedures.

A refinement of the investigative progress into the composition of coins beyond that of merely establishing their intrinsic values in relation to proportions of precious metals to adulterants, is the identification of mineral sources. To identify the place of origin of coin metal is to open up a line of research into trade routes and political alignments which are otherwise unrecorded. There are limitations on the scope of this work because coins themselves often provide the material for later generations of coins. Remelting can so mix the constituents of a coinage as to make accurate sourcing impossible. However, in the early stages of coinage, for instance, sourcing of raw materials may be possible.

Since silver is far and away the most important metal of early coinage it is fortunate that lead isotope analysis is available as an investigative tool. The investigation of lead isotopes proceeds from the fact that lead ores contain the four stable isotopes of lead in varying proportions. These proportions depend on the geological environment in which the ores have formed in the earth's crust and the manner in which they have been originally extruded from the magmatic core.

The isotope 'finger print' of the ore does not change when it is converted to metal. Since almost all silver was, until recently, extracted from lead, and since all silver contains a proportion of lead, it is possible to investigate the lead isotopes in silver coins in order to match their isotopic 'finger prints' with that of known sources of silver. The range of coinage which can be examined extends to leaded bronzes as well as silver issues. This work is in its infancy but has already produced surprising, and numismatically contentious, results when applied to the fifth-century BC Greek coinage, suggesting a surprising number of sources for coining metal and thus a complex series of political or trade relationships between those who owned mineral resources and those who produced coins from them.[8]

One further non-destructive method exists which has a history nearly as long as coinage itself.

Specific gravity

It seems to be almost redundant to reiterate the schoolboy definition of Archimedes' principle which is exemplified every time one puts a teaspoon into an already overfull coffee cup – that when a body is immersed in a liquid it displaces an equal weight of the liquid. Because metals differ in their volume-to-weight ratios it is possible to establish the purity of a material, effectively gold and silver, by checking its volume-to-weight ratio against a set of empirical standards. The application of specific gravity determination to the establishment of coin constituents has been a recent revival of the process. This revival owes its origin to the development of highly accurate experimental procedures which have overcome the problems of establishing the specific gravity of alloys or bimetallic coins.

Specific gravity determination is restricted to assessing proportions of silver to gold or gold to copper. Silver/copper determinations are not possible. This is because the specific gravities of silver and copper are so close as to make accurate estimation of their relative proportions difficult. In reality all alloys contain an element of copper, and an empirical formula has been devised which allows for the depressing effect of the presence of this element on the calculation of the content of silver in relation to, say, gold.[9]

Specific gravity determination has an advantage over the other methods outlined above in that it is completely non-destructive and can be deployed *in situ* where the coins are housed. For these reasons this was the method adopted to establish the fineness, and thus the relative date, of the coins from Sutton Hoo burial (*see p. 86*). Besides the 37 coins and the five blanks and billets from the ship, 750 other examples of the coinage were analysed from European collections. The method is speedy, cheap and simple:

1. The coin is weighed in air.
2. The coin is weighed in a liquid (Perfluoro-1-methyl decalin, which has a low surface tension)
3. The wire used to suspend the coin in the liquid is weighed.
4. The temperature of the liquid (viscosity varies with temperature) is ascertained.

From these determinations the specific gravity of the coin is calculated by the formula:

$$\frac{\text{Wt. of coin in air} \times \text{specific gravity of liquid}}{[(\text{Wt. of coin in air}) - (\text{Wt. of coin in liquid})]} = \text{Specific gravity of coin}$$

Since specific gravity is related directly to purity, the amount of gold in the Sutton Hoo coins could be calculated with allowance being made for the presence of copper.

Correlation between the results obtained by the various methods outlined above shows that each has its uses and that the choice of analytical technique may be determined by access to suitable experimental facilities. Experiments using all available methods have been conducted and these give good agreement between the various methods or produce divergent results which are explicable. Figure 19 reproduces the results of the testing of six gold and six silver coins by a number of investigative methods: specific gravity (1), neutron activation of the whole coin (2), neutron activation of a streak (3), XRF (4), touchstone (5), fire assay (6) and chemical analysis (7). The discrepant results for the gold coins BML3 and BML5 arise because, in the former, a high percentage of copper is present which has affected the specific gravity calculation and in the latter the streak for neutron activation analysis was found to have been taken from a coin which had been gilded. In the silver coins the 'streak' method has again produced a discrepant result (BML5) and the presence of copper had distorted the reading obtained for BML3 by the specific gravity method. It is of interest to note that the touchstone analysis, the method used in antiquity and the medieval period, is in agreement with the modern science based methods.

Analytical work has made available a whole range of new information. Sources of raw materials, metrological standards and metalurgical problems can now be investigated and understood. It is to be hoped that it is of some comfort to the moneyers employed by Henry I who suffered castration as punishment, in 1124, for issuing adulterated money that an electron microprobe investigation of their coins has proved them innocent.

In discussing the methods employed in the analysis of coins we have stressed that the elimination of superficial deposits and corrosion products is of paramount importance. These are also the problems which are faced by conservators.

The conservation of coins presents a number of conflicts of

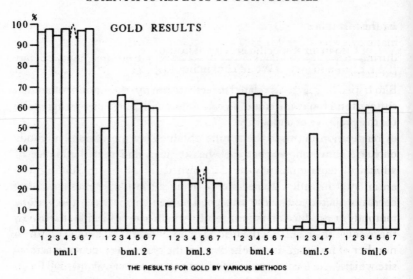

THE RESULTS FOR GOLD BY VARIOUS METHODS

KEY: 1. Specific-gravity method. 2. Neutron activation of the whole coin. 3. Neutron activation of 'streaks'.

4. X-ray flourescence (Milliprobe). 5. Touchstone 6. Fire assay. 7. Chemical analysis.

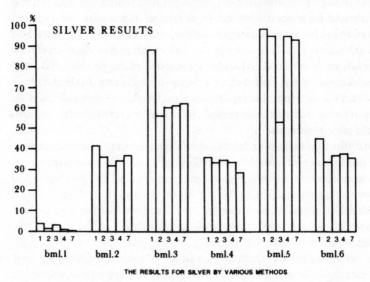

THE RESULTS FOR SILVER BY VARIOUS METHODS

KEY: 1. Specific-gravity method 2. Neutron activation of the whole coin 3. Neutron activation of 'streaks'.

4. X-ray flourescence.(Milliprobe). 7. Chemical analysis.

19. Multiple technique analysis of gold and silver coinage (after Oddy).

138

interest.[10] The site director is naturally anxious to assess the numismatic evidence from his excavation at the earliest moment, if possible during the course of the excavation itself. Coins always create excitement when they are found and the natural reaction of the finder is to try to identify them, and this is sometimes possible if they have not suffered post-depositional damage. Some environments are non-corrosive and with a little practice any archaeologist can master the art of reading a coin inscription and form an estimate of its production date. He will thus have some sort of working framework of dating in which to conduct his research. Unfortunately, most excavated coins are in a deplorable condition, thickly encrusted with a hard shell of corrosion products inextricably mixed with soil and stones. The temptation to try to clean these on site should always be resisted unless the excavation is equipped with the right facilities and a conservator. A number of methods have been used in the past to aid identification on site which have long-term destabilising effects on coins and may result in their eventual dissolution. Coins should never be treated with acids, washed in anything but distilled or deionised water or attacked with abrasives or stiff brushes. Some coins are in such fragile condition that they should be treated with the same lifting techniques as any other class of delicate object encountered during the excavation. Where acid soils are encountered the excavator should be prepared to deal with coins which have been reduced to a porous mass which retains the shape of the original coin but which will disintegrate if disturbed. In these cases the coin should be lifted with a block of soil and retained in its environment until conservation can take place. In no circumstances should cleaning be attempted on such material. Any such misguided efforts will quickly eliminate the most affected area of the coin – the surface layers – and with the destruction of these layers the obverse and reverse images of the coin type will disappear, leaving a residual core of unidentifiable metal.

The laboratory conservation of coins is a subject in which sharp controversy has arisen between the conservators who carry out this important work and numismatists. The former treat coins as an aspect of the scientific conservation of metals in general whilst the numismatists catalogue, classify and study coins as the raw material for the advancement of their own branch of learning.

The conflict arises from the numismatist's absolute need to identify coins down to the minutest detail, and for this it is essential that coins submitted for study should be in a good condition. The sort of detail which is required includes complete legibility of types, inscriptions, mintmarks and any symbols or letters which appear as elements of the overall design of the coin. Such revelation may call for very drastic removal of the deposits and corrosion products which have formed on the coin during its burial in the soil. Unfortunately the removal of these deposits may fundamentally change the nature of the coin. We have already discussed the losses which can be sustained by the body of the coin in time – the leaching out of copper near the surface, the formation of corrosion products within the body of the coin and the migration of core material to the periphery of the flan. Cleaning can remove all traces of these migrating constituents, but it can also remove evidence of the original appearance of the coin. Let us suppose that the coin, when issued, had a bright silvery appearance and that this was achieved by a plating process, such as tinning, which produced a superficial layer which formed a separate phase from the body of the coin itself. Drastic cleaning would certainly remove such evidence. The same result would be achieved if a coin with a gilt foil covering were drastically treated. Conservators see that it is their ethical duty to preserve such evidence; numismatists agree with them wholeheartedly but point out that the huge mass of coins from excavations present a body of material which is already well understood through analyses, and that the overwhelming need is to identify this coinage, in detail, for its chronological value to the excavation rather than for its compositional information, or for the secondary purpose of determining the processes of the formation of corrosion products.

Virtually no other class of metal objects from excavations presents the same identification problems as coins. Pots, pans and fibulae can be identified even in extremely corroded condition. Iron objects, though subject to severe corrosion, normally retain their shape, but a corroded and encrusted coin is like an unopened book. It is not until the pages are opened and the print is visible that we know whether we are dealing with Agatha Christie or Ammianus Marcellinus. It is, therefore, a cause of considerable irritation when the numismatist receives from the conservation laboratory an object which is a stabilised mass of corrosion in which lurks the object of his real interest, the coin itself.

Problems arise because archaeologists and numismatists use the same words but in different senses in their own specific vocabularies. It should be understood that 'conservation' is not the same thing as 'cleaning'. An uncleaned coin which presents problems of identification to the numismatist may be in a good state of conservation as far as the conservator is concerned. Ideally the three parties involved in an excavation's coinage problems, the excavator, conservator and numismatist, work in close co-operation, with the latter indicating what degree of cleaning is necessary for him to fulfil his task of identification. This can often be achieved from a small area of the coin surface, and a standard catalogue reference achieved with only the minimum use of precious conservation resources in unnecessary work.

Many excavations conducted by archaeologists outside their own country deploy a numismatist on the staff and this procedure is advised not only where local laws require excavated material to stay on the site of its discovery or within its country of origin but also where soil conditions are known to be detrimental to the preservation of metal artefacts. In these conditions coins are often in a very fragile condition and should be seen by the numismatist before any conservation takes place. In acid soil conditions a coin may appear to be intact when in reality it is simply a powdery mass of copper carbonate or silver chloride which retains all of the features of a coin until it is lefted from the soil, at which point disintegration occurs. Cataloguing in the field is needed in these conditions.

Conservation methods vary with the composition and condition of the coin to be treated. As far as composition is concerned this is an area where numismatic advice can be offered to the conservator. Generally speaking current conservation practice eschews the use of chemical solvents to extract the coin from its matrix of corrosion products in favour of mechanical cleaning.

Mechanical cleaning involves the removal of corrosion products by the use of dental picks and the Vibratool. The latter is a mechanical hammer, normally used in engraving glass and metals, which can be fitted with a needle which strikes the coin at great pressure and at a rate of several thousand blows per minute. In skilled hands this equipment can release a coin from its encasing mass of carbonate and cuprite corrosion. The problem is that such treatment can change the surface of a coin quite radically by chipping pieces from lettering and re-engraving fine details. These details are exactly the small features which are closely investigated in die studies, and morphological changes to the coin during the process of preservation must be avoided. Although a numismatist may have a very good idea of what the corrosion is hiding, this is probably not true of the conservator, who may have very little idea of what is lurking below the obscuring encrustation. So we have an impasse – conservators abjure chemical cleaning and numismatists dislike the mechanical method.

However, the archaeologist working in areas where there are no conservation facilities and where there is a prohibition on the removal of excavated finds may need to have coins cleaned in the field. In the absence of an on-site conservator and/or numismatist, advice and training should always be obtained before embarking upon the excavation. There are a number of chemical treatments available for dealing with superficial corrosion of base metal and silver coins and an excavator contemplating the treatment of coins in the field would need to be supplied with these and be fully briefed on their use by a conservation expert. It should be stressed that the use of such reagents, whilst giving immediate access to the identification of the coins, also exposes them to further deterioration. Full conservation procedures should always follow cleaning in order to ensure the long-term preservation of the object treated.

Faced by the problem of having no resources for cataloguing and study in the field, the archaeologist overseas must record his coin finds in a way that will allow them to be closely studied in another place. The most obvious recording method is by photography but this is also the least satisfactory. Coin photography is in itself an art which calls for long practice and wide experience in order to capture on film what the human eye can see. It is better to make a cast of the coins on site or to make moulds from which casts can later be obtained.

The simplest method of preparing casts is to make a mould of the coin by pressing it into the surface of a pad of softened plasticine. The surface of the pad should be rubbed with talc, which acts as a releasing agent and stops the coin sticking in the mould. A cream-thick mixture of dental plaster is prepared and spooned into the mould which should be gently shaken from side to side to expel air bubbles. When the cast is dry it can be disengaged from the mould. It is often convenient to use the back of the cast to record such details as the registration number of the coin. Paired casts of the obverse and reverse of a single coin can be mounted on a card for ease of handling.

Plasticine moulds can be prepared and casts made at a later date but the mould material is liable to distortion in high temperatures as it

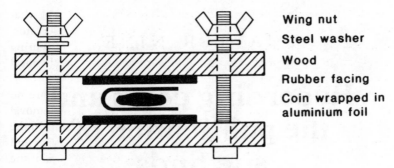

Wing nut
Steel washer
Wood
Rubber facing
Coin wrapped in
aluminium foil

20. Cliché moulding apparatus.

softens. An alternative, which is more portable and quicker to prepare, is the cliché mould (*Plate 6 :6,7,8*). A thickness of aluminium foil (kitchen foil) is folded round the coin; this package is then placed between two rubber pads and pressure applied. A simple press is used to apply sufficient pressure. A suitable apparatus can be made with two short wooden slats which are closed together by an arrangement of screws and winged nuts (*Figure 20*). The impression of the coin produced by the cliché method can be read directly or used as a mould to make a cast. Aluminium foil clichés are indestructable, but need careful storage so as not to erase the impression of the coin. Naturally, care should be taken in the choice of coins submitted to this process. The pressure needed to replicate all of the features of a coin in the foil is quite high and thin or twisted coins may be seriously damaged or broken.

CHAPTER NINE

Recording coins and the publication of site finds

It has been constantly stressed that any work in the field of numismatics calls for very high standards of accuracy. Coins must be identified and described with the closest attention to detail; equally, the provenance must be ascertained and doubtful material, whether deposited by ignorance or, not infrequently, malice, eliminated from the scholar's record. There are all sorts of traps to be avoided, not least that created by the widespread dispersal of good imitations of ancient and medieval coins which are sold by museums to visitors or circulated by companies as publicity gifts. These are already creeping into local museums' regional coin records. Some have even been mischievously put into important contexts on excavations, all of which means that recording must be of the highest possible standard.

On an archaeological site the recording of coins should follow the normal procedures established to locate and fix the position of all archaeological small finds. The coin should be recorded in its exact context and the record of the findspot always travel with the coin. On site the archaeologist will record the unique identification of the feature in which the coin is found, whether this be a level, pit or other recognisable ambience which is physically distinct from the matrix in which it is embedded. In addition the three-dimensional co-ordinates of the coin will be recorded, its vertical position measured from an established datum point and its horizontal location fixed within the overall grid of the site. Only when these records have been made should the coin be removed from its context.

The record of a coin's findspot should be kept in at least two separate places, in the register of finds and in the site feature records, whether this be a site book, feature record sheet or a direct input to a computer. It is normal practice to bag coins individually in small paper or plastic envelopes; these containers should bear an indelible record of the context from which the coin has been taken as well as its find registration number. As physical deterioration may accelerate in conditions of site storage, coin bags, if plastic, should be ventilated. A quantity of silica gel in the storage container of the coins helps to minimise the effects of damp and humidity.

Often coins are in very poor physical condition and show clear signs of deterioration, with patches of green copper chloride corrosion or heavy incrustations of silver chloride or copper carbonate. As we have noted, the treatment of these chemical problems should be reserved for the laboratory; the temptation to scrape away corrosion products to establish on-site identification should always be resisted, since such action can set up irreversible processes of decay in the coin. Despite near obscurity of design and detail, coin experts familiar with coins from long experience of handling large numbers of them from all sorts of environments and in a variety of desperate conditions, can often supply the excavator with dating on site without the need for the drastic destabilisation of what may be a very fragile object.

Like other experts who contribute to excavation reports but who do not control the final product, numismatists sometimes express exasperation at the way in which their contribution has been treated. The weeks of careful cataloguing, the meticulous descriptions, the tedious identification of common coins of little real numismatic interest often seems to amount to very little in the final analysis. If this is ever the case it is entirely the fault of the numismatist whose duty should be to co-operate with the archaeologist at the earliest stage of the excavation and to continue this co-operation through all stages up to the publication of the final report of the excavation. This process will stop the numismatist, as much as the archaeologist, from jumping to false conclusions based exclusively on coins where there is other evidence, perhaps ceramic or epigraphic, which is incompatible with his own deductions. For instance it is normally the practice to send coins of different series to different specialists. In these circumstances it is no good at all for the Roman specialist to build up a chronological scheme if down the road a medieval specialist is working on coins from the same site and these coins are found in contexts which the Romanist thinks of as completely within the Roman period. Clearly the whole body of coin and other evidence must be assessed before hasty conclusions are reached.

The publication of coins from archaeological sites may take a number of forms. Such publication usually differs from the publication of coins in purely numismatic literature because of the need for brevity and the need to unite the description of the individual coin with the specific context from which it derives. However, it is the formal numismatic publication which sets the ultimate standard and a formal vocabulary of description has been evolved which can intimidate the non-specialist.

In describing coins, numismatists use a specialised vocabulary to indicate the various components which go to make up the coin. The shaped piece of metal on which the coin design is imposed is called the *blank* or *flan* (*Plate 7 :2*). The flan is struck with a pair of *dies* (*Plate 7 :1*) with which the normally bifacial design is imposed on the metal. Of the two sides of the coin, that which bears the portrait is the *obverse* (appreviated to obv.) and the side which bears the *type*, or design, is the *reverse* (abbreviated to rev.). The rotational angle between the face of the upper die and the face of the lower is called the *die axis*. The angle of the die axis is indicated by representing the obverse as an arrow pointing at a twelve o'clock position with an arrow representing the reverse die's position superimposed upon it thus:

The coin itself may bear an obverse and reverse *legend* or be anepigraphic. Included with the reverse legend, which is often descriptive of the type, may be letters or figures in the *field* of the coin, that is the area within the encircling reverse legend. These may be termed *fieldmarks* and can consist of sequence letters, numbers or symbols, the significance of which are now largely lost (*Plate 8 :1*). In the Greek series the reverse may also carry the monogram of the issuing mint and of the magistrate responsible for the emission (*Plate 7 :3*). Often the reverse type is set on a groundline which creates a small lunate space at the bottom of the coin. This space, the *exergue*, may be occupied by a date (*Plate 8 :2*) or by a *mintmark* (abbreviated mm.). The mintmark may be in the form of an abbreviation of the name of the town in which the mint is located and may additionally incorporate an indication of the mint workship. or *officina*, responsible for the production of the individual coin. Medieval coins often incorporate the name of the mint as a direct statement as part of the reverse legend, together with the name of the moneyer responsible for striking the coin (*Plate 8 : 3, 4*). Medieval English coins used a large series of symbols incorporated in the reverse legend to indicate the mint and probably the person responsible for their production in order that any defects could be laid at the door of the defaulting worker or mint officer.

Sometimes things went wrong. Until very recently coins were hand struck and once in a while a struck coin remained adhering to the upper, movable, die instead of falling away on striking into the heap of newly made coins. This struck coin is then used to strike the next blank placed on the lower, head, die. The result is the production of a *brockage* in which a coin is produced with a perfectly normal obverse and an incuse head for its reverse (*Plate 7 : 4*). Occasionally a new coin will be struck on a pre-existing one instead of on a new blank in such a way that the new striking fails to obliterate the old coin, so that an *undertype* is visible. *Overstrikes* of this kind are very valuable aids in establishing the relative dates of otherwise undated issues (*Plate 8 : 5, 6, 7, 8*). Not to be confused with this process is the one in which more than one attempt is made to strike a coin and where the die shifts across the face of the blank between blows, or the blank itself moves in relation to the die. In either event a double impression is created as a result of the coin being *doublestruck* (*Plate 8 : 9*).

All of these pieces of information will be recorded by the numismatist, with each period and series of coins sharing in a common body of numismatic descriptive conventions, supplemented by those specific to individual series. For instance, in the Roman series, where the elaboration of fieldmarks and mintmarks becomes very complex in the fourth century, it is sometimes necessary to illustrate the disposition of the various subsidiary letters and figures. For this a conventional system has been evolved: the right and left hand sides of the reverse are represented as divided by a vertical line, and the exergue by a horizontal in the form of an upside down letter T. All coin descriptions are related to the viewer, so that right and left are as seen when looking at the coin. A typical depiction of a coin using this sytem can be drawn from the early fourth century where the coins issued by the mint of Alexandria in 316 bore the field- and mintmarks disposed around the pictorial elements of the reverse. Disposing of the latter, the convention gives a diagrammatic version of the ancillary elements of the type:

Most coin series can now boast standard reference catalogues so that full description is not always necessary, and reference can be made to the appropriate catalogue entry where the extended descriptive details are available. Of course it does not follow that because a series of coins is arranged in an impressive catalogue they are necessarily accurately dated, either relatively or absolutely, or even that they are correctly attributed. Coin studies are dynamic and an archaeologist basing a chronology on such entries would be very foolish indeed if he did not check with a specialist to see whether or not there had been any reattribution or redating since the appearance of the catalogue. For instance, in the British Celtic series all of the coins attributed to the Brigantes have been correctly reattributed to the tribe of the Coritani, though the old attribution continued to appear in archaeological works for some time after the change had been published in the numismatic literature.

Catalogues are normally arranged in chronological order, though this order may be diffused and confusing to the non-specialist. Arrangement may be primarily by issuer and then by descending order of denomination. In the Roman series the standard catalogue, Roman Imperial Coinage, is arranged in a number of ways. Early volumes divided coins into precious metal and base metal issues and thus divorced contemporary issues from each other. Later volumes brought the material more closely together but published them under the issuing mints rather than rulers, because similar issues were struck at a number of mints and a single type can appear in a number of places. In the circumstances, it is vital to assign the coin accurately to a mint either by reading the mintmark or by stylistic criteria before cataloguing can proceed.

In the past, archaeological studies of coins were impeded by very poor publication standards. Archaeologists considered it sufficient to publish only the coins which they thought of as 'archaeologically significant', that is, stratified coins which reinforced the chronological framework of the excavation report. Now unstratified coins do not fall out of the sky, they are, as we have seen, a very important part of the site record. How they reached their resting place is a point which should be considered. For instance, the presence of many Roman coins in a medieval structure may indicate that an unsuspected Roman site is nearby from which levelling material has been obtained.

Unhelpful coin lists, in which the material is listed simply by issuer with no reference to types, are now rare but do still appear. This sort of publication impedes the archaeologist as much as the numismatist and may completely obscure the finer points of chronological and economic information invested in the coins. There is only one standard of publication and that can be summed up as 'all of the information, all of the time'. Selective publication is a policy currently being advocated because full publication makes great demands on the specialist's time and is a financial burden because of publication costs. Such a policy should be strongly resisted. As a scientist the archaeologist is duty bound to present his results with the supporting evidence for critical scrutiny not just by his immediate colleagues but by future generations of scholars who may not have access to the material data on which the report is based.

Even without such highminded considerations, practicality demands full publication as an index to archived material from a site. A case in point arose recently when the coin display from a museum crashed to the ground when it was being removed to new premises. The display included, among others, all of the coins from a major site. Only by relating each coin in the fully detailed lists published in the excavation report could the site coins be recovered from the shambles of the accident.

What should be the norm? Ideally each coin should be recorded with full obverse and reverse legends. The legends should be spelled out as they appear on the coin, including any stops between words or breaks in the legend. Incomplete legends should be restored when this can be done with confidence. Let us exemplify all this from a coin of the notably prolix and prolific emperor Trajan. It will be convenient to reproduce the details on the sort of catalogue card which many workers use to record individual coins and which can later be deposited as an archive and index of the coins themselves:

PIERCEBRIDGE	No. **89**
DERE STREET, 1974	RIC. **142**
	BMC.
	LRBC.1.
Ruler: **TRAJAN**	LRBC.2.
Denom. **DENARIUS**	Obv. [**IMP TRAIANO AVG GER DAC PM TR P**]
"In first re-metalling of Dere St."	Rev. **COS V PP SPQR OPTIMO PRINC**
	Issue date: **103–11**
	Condition: **VW/VW**

The catalogue entry tells us a number of things: the site and the sub-area of the site in which the coin was found, together with the small find registration number. We also have the reference number to this issue in the standard catalogue of the series, Roman Imperial Coinage (RIC). The denomination is also recorded, since the standard catalogue sometimes lists different denominations under the same number. Any comments culled from the excavator or his records is included on the index card. This information will be of use to the numismatist in compiling his report and to future users of the archive. Observe and reverse legends are spelled out as given on the coin. The square brackets around the obverse legend indicate that it is illegible but can be restored with confidence. Any field or mintmarks would be recorded following the reverse description. The issue date is that covered by the years of Trajan's fifth consulship. The condition of the coin is that in which it was at the moment of loss; subsequent corrosion is ignored in trying to ascertain this state. Different workers have slightly different ways of indicating the condition. In the present example the indication is that the obverse is very worn, as is the reverse. A range of conditions, all ultimately subjective, may be evident:

UW – Unworn
SW – Slightly worn

W – Worn
VW – Very worn
EW – Extremely worn

Whilst of no absolute chronological value, the condition of wear should be recorded to give a general impression of the amount of use seen by the coins overall. All of the information contained by the catalogue card can be transferred to computer, if necessary, with its concommitant ease of manipulating the report coin list into the order required for publication, be it chronological, feature by feature or both. Cataloguing directly on to computer, whilst attractive in theory, presents practical problems of access in the field and is actually physically difficult because it is suprisingly hard to manipulate a computer keyboard whilst consulting a complex and bulky coin catalogue volume.

The information transferred from the catalogue card to the published account may, despite all advice to the contrary, have to be printed in an abbreviated form. The simplest form of publication is by the standard catalogue reference. In the instance quoted above, the coin of Trajan would simply be listed as RIC 142, leaving a reader with further interest in the matter to consult the full catalogue for himself to ascertain the denomination, type and date of issue. However, numbers have a way of going astray between proof correcting and printing and it may be thought prudent to give an indication of the type with the catalogue number. In this case the entry would read RIC 142 (Dacia), referring to the most prominent feature of the reverse type. Coins which cannot be catalogued to a specific reference can be dealt with by the excellent system devised by Richard Reece which economically indicates the degree of closeness a less than fully identifiable coin bears to a fully identifiable type. In the case of our Trajanic coin uncertainty would be shown by cataloguing it as 'as RIC 142'. The system can be extended to the notorious problem of copies in which bungled types and legends are so frequent as to make exact ascription to prototype difficult. Where certainty exists a coin is denoted 'copy of 142' and where uncertainty 'copy as 142'.

There are a number of methods of relating individual coins to the excavation contexts from which they derive. A popular system is to refer from a chronological catalogue, in which all of the site's coins are listed in the order of their dates of issue with a running number

TIBERIUS II

26 September 578 — 14 August 582

NO.	WT.	DIAM.	AXIS	OBVERSE	REVERSE	DATE	REF.
				Copper			
				CONSTANTINOPLE			
				FOLLIS			
				Consular bust facing; crown with cross; in r., mappa; in l., eagle-tipped scepter with cross above.	M Above, cross. To l., A N N O In ex., CON		
521	?–7.8	25–29	\	]ONS TAN[	To r., Ч After CON, Δ	579	*11 d.3
522	9.1–8.8	26	↓	Illeg.	Ч Є	579/80	R930
523	12.6–12.5	28–29	↑	DMϹIbCON STAN[ ]ΛV[	ЧI Γ	580/1	W*31
524	?–6.5	24–28	?	Illeg.	[ЧI] ?	[580/1]	
525	?–6.9	(17)–30	↙	o M[	? Δ	579–582	
				HALF FOLLIS			
				Armored bust facing; in r., gl. cr.	XX Above, cross. In ex., CON		
526	6.2–6.0	21–23	↙	→ MTIb C ONSTГГAV	After CON, B	579–582	*17b.2 var.
527	?–6.3	23–24	↙	Illeg.	Γ	579–582	W*45
				DECANUMMIUM			
				Bust facing, cuirass; crown with cross.	I To l. & r., stars. In ex., CON		
528	?–2.9	17–20	↓	]N[ ] [ ]RPP Ν	Stars, *	578	*18.1

NO.	AREA	GRID		LEVEL	NOTES	FIND DATE
521	HoB	E 30	S 60	ca. 96.3–96.92		8/24/59
522	SynFc	E 100	N ?–10	96.9–97.5	In fill	8/14/62
523	MTE	E 52	S 124.5	102		8/20/64
524	BS–W 9	W 30.2–32.3	S 0–4.8	96.8–97.9	Sifting	7/9/59
525	BS–E 13	E 75.9–80.3	S 0.1–4	96.4–96.6		8/26/62
526	PN	W 250	S 360	89.3 (L)		7/7/61
527	BS–E 10	E 62.5–63	S 2.65	96.3	Hoard S	8/6/67
528	BS–E 16	E 91.3–95.8	S 0–4	96.4		8/23/63

21. Sardis excavation coin record system.

attached, to a list of features or contexts which yielded coins. A list of the features is then constructed with the numbered coins incorporated so that the reader can both see the overall picture of the coins and relate back to them from the excavation details thus:

Phase IVB (Stone barrack replacing timber building of Phase IVA)
   Coins. 4, 9, 37, 46

Phase VII (Make up of floors of Building B)
Coins. 29, 31, 70, 81, 88

A very good method of publication, but also a very expensive one, is that adopted in the report on the Byzantine coins from the excavations at Sardis (*Figure 21*).[1] Here each coin is fully described and the excavation details are related to the individual coins in a numerically parallel sub-text. On very large excavations, like those of urban sites in the Mediterranean, listing by major features may be needed where these features are actual buildings with long histories of use and coin activity. It may be best to treat each context as a separate coin report rather than lead the reader back and forth through a list of several thousand coins derived from the whole site.

Depending on the policy of the excavator, or more probably his sponsors, the coin publication will appear as an integral part of an excavation report or form a separate publication. In either event the numismatist would expect to be given sufficient scope to discuss the coins and their fuller aspects in an economic, regional or purely typological context. Inevitably the suggestion will be made that the numismatic detail should be consigned to archive and that only an abstract of evidence be published or that the full report should be presented on microfiche. Both suggestions should be resisted. Microfiche is a typical invention of abstract rationalisation which takes not the slightest notice of the convenience of the user nor the improbability of the average reader having access to a reader, even if the wretched plastic sheets, on which scores of pages of text have been reduced microscopically, have survived intact in the volume. Whilst not advocating a return to the illuminated manuscript, a little bit of stubborn conservatism may be looked upon gratefully by future generations.

References, notes
and bibliography

General works

There is a formidable number of specialised works on numismatics but very few general works which outline the principles of numismatic study without getting over-involved with specific problems. An exception is P. Grierson *Numismatics* (1975). A general overview of coinage throughout the world and of all periods will be found in R.S.G. Carson *Coins, ancient, mediaeval and modern*. A wide-ranging view of medieval and early modern coinage within a framework of historical, economic and social events will be found in J. Porteous *Coins in history* (1969). Greek and Roman coins have been subject to a number of general studies; among the most up to date and accessible are C. Kraay *Archaic and classical Greek coins* (Cambridge, 1976), G.K. Jenkins *Ancient Greek coins* (1972), J.P.C. Kent *Roman coins* (1978) and R.A.G. Carson *A guide to the principal coins of the Romans* (1978/82).

Chapter 1

1. *Primitive money* The extraordinarily wide range of objects used in trade, exchange and barter are dealt with in their ethnographic and anthropological contexts in J.C. Quiggin *Primitive money* (1949)
2. *Greek coin issues* The periodicity of Greek coin issue is dealt with by C. Kraay *Archaic and classical Greek coins*, loc. cit. and by K. Rutter 'Early Greek coinage and the influence of the Athenian state' in B. Cunnliffe ed. *Coinage and society in Britain and Gaul : some current problems* (1981).
3. Mouchmov, N.A. *Le grand tresor numismatique de Reka Devnia (Marcianopolis) (Sofia, 1939)*
4. Griffith, G.T. *The mercenaries of the Hellenistic world* (1935).
5. The extravagant behaviour of Louernios, who was in deep political

difficulties at the time so that his behaviour may not have been entirely characteristic of all Celtic chieftans, is recounted in Posidonius' 'Celtic Ethnography' *via* Athenaeus. (*See below p. 156.*)

6. Cunliffe, B.W. *Hengistbury Head* (1978)

7. Sellwood, D. *An introduction to the coinage of Parthia* 2nd ed. (1980)

8. Oddy, W. A. and Munro-Hay, S. C. 'The specific gravity analysis of the gold coins in Aksum' in Oddy, W.A. and Metcalf, D. eds. *Metallurgy in numismatics* (1980). A systematic listing of the coinage of Aksum with a full discussion of the chronological problems posed by this coinage is now to be found in S.C. Munro-Hay *The coinage of Aksum* (1984)

9. North, J.J. *English hammered coinage* (1960)

Chapter 2

1. Price, M.J. and Trell, B. *Coins and their cities: architecture on the ancient coins of Greece, Rome and Palestine* (1977)

2. Rainbird, J.S. and Sear, F.B. 'A possible description of the Macellum Magnum of Nero' *Papers of the British School of Rome*, XXXIX, 1971, 40–47

3. Milne, J.B. *University of Oxford Ashmolean Museum: catalogue of Alexandrian coins* (Oxford, 1971). The changes which can be observed in the form of the Pharos between the reign of Hadrian and his successor Pius are found on Milne 1381 and 1841. The former coin, dating to AD 134, shows the lighthouse as a four sided tower with a lantern on the top and with a door at the foot on one side. On the coinage of Pius issued in 145, the entrance has been shifted to a position part way up the tower and access is by means of a staircase leading up to the new door

4. Ragette, F. *Baalbek* (1980)

5. *Pepys Diary* ed. R. Latham and W. Matthews (1974) 2/224, 6/326. Although the coin of the Commonwealth was demonetised for trade and private transactions the state was prepared to accept it in payment of taxes until May 1, 1662, thus tempering political animosity with financial practicality.

6. Casey, P.J. 'Tradition and innovation in the coinage of Carausius and Allectis', in Munby, J. and Henig, M. eds. *Roman life and art in Britain* (Oxford, 1977)

7. Bertele, T. *Numismatique byzantine* (Wetteren, 1978)

8. Lyon, S. 'Some problems of interpreting Anglo-Saxon coinage' *Anglo-Saxon England*, 5, 1976

Chapter 3

1. Milne, J.G. *loc. cit.*

2a. Casey, P.J. 'Constantine the Great in Britain – the evidence of the coinage of the mint of London, AD 312–314' in J. Bird *et al*, eds. *Collectanea Londiniensia: studies in London archaeology and history presented to Ralph Merrifield* (1978)

2b. Eusebius *Oratio de laudibus Constantini*. ed. I.A. Heikel. Trans. H. Wace and P. Schaff. *A select library of Nicene and post-Nicene fathers* Vol. I (Oxford, 1895)

3. Casey, P.J. 'The coins from the excavations at High Rochester in 1852 and 1856' *Arch. Aeliana*, 5th ser. VIII, 1980, 75–89

4–6. *Late Roman coinage in north Wales*. Besides the coins from Caernarfon there are similar finds from what appears to be a late Roman coastal defence tower at Holyhead on the island of Anglesey (Crew, forthcoming) and from an as yet undefined site called Llys Awal in North Wales. Older finds from the fort of Caerhun, Conway, may also fit into this emerging pattern of post-Maximus military occupation. The text of Gildas may be conveniently studied in *De exidio Britonum*, edited and translated by M. Winterbottom (1978). The revision of the place of Maximus in Britain is, found in Casey, P.J. 'Magnus Maximus in Britain: a reappraisal in Casey, P.J. ed. *The end of Roman Britain* (Oxford, 1979).

7. Tacitus *De vita Agricolae* ed. R. M. Ogilvie and I. A. Richmond (Oxford, 1967)

8. Buttrey, T. V. *Documentary evidence for the chronology of the Flavian titulature.* (Meisenheim am Glan, 1980)

9. Procopius *The secret history* Loeb ed. trans. H. B. Dewing

10. Casey, P. J. 'Justinian and the *limitanei*' in Breeze, D. ed. *Studies presented to J.C. Mann* (forthcoming)

11. Just about everything that we know about Celtic life is derived from Caesar and Posidonius. The sources are conveniently collected and translated in J.J. Tierney 'The Celtic ethnography of Posidonius' *Procs. Royal Irish Academy, 60, 1960, 5–275*

12. Nash, D. 'Coinage and state development in Central Gaul' in Cunliffe, B. ed. *Coinage and society in Britain and Gaul loc cit.*

13. *Celtic coinage* The most convenient overall listing of Celtic coinage types in Britain is R.P. Mack *The coinage of ancient Britain* 3rd ed. (1975)

Chapter 4

1. *Brixellum (Modena) Hoard.* Crawford, M.J. *Roman republican coin hoards* (1969)

2. *Pepys diary loc cit.* 8/263–4, 8/472–5.

3. Bastien, P. and Metzger, C. *Le tresor de Beaurains (dit d'Arras)* (Wetteren, 1977)

4. Hendy, M.F. 'The Gornoslav hoard, the emperor Frederick I and the

monastery of Bachkovo' in C.N.L. Brooke ed. *Studies in numismatic method presented to Philip Grierson* (Cambridge, 1983)

5. Crawford, M.J. *Roman republican coin hoards* (Cambridge, 1974)

6. Brown, I.D. and Dolley, M. *Coin hoards of Great Britain and Ireland, 1500–1967* (1971)

7. Kent, J.C.P. 'Interpreting coin finds' in Casey, P.J. and Reece, R. eds. *Coins and the archaeologist* (Oxford, 1974)

8. Crawford, M.J. *The Roman republic* (1978) and more fully in *Papers of the British School of Rome*, XXXVI, 1969, 79ff.

9. Brown, I.D. and Dolley, M. *Coin hoards of Great Britain.*

10. Frere, S.S. *Britannia : a history of Roman Britain* 2nd ed. (1974) p.215

11. Mattingly, H. 'The great Dorchester hoard' *Num. Chron.*, 5th ser., XIX, 1939, 21–61

Chapter 5

1. Tacitus *De vita Agricolae* ed Ogilvie and Richmond *loc cit.*

2. Philips, D. *Excavations below the Minster at York.* (forthcoming). This information is given with the kind consent of the excavator.

Chapter 6

1. Thompson, M. *The Athenian agora ... Vol. 2. Greek, Roman, Byzantine and Crusader coins* (Princeton, 1954)

2. Wheeler, R.E.M. and T.V. *Verulamium : a Belgic and two Roman cities* (1936). For the latest consideration of the coins from Verulamium, which includes those found by Wheeler, casual finds from the site and those derived from the latest large-scale excavations, see R. Reece 'The coins' in S.S. Frere *Verulamium excavations Vol. III* (Oxford, 1984)

3. Gillam, J. 'The Roman forts at Corbridge' *Arch. Aeliana, 5th ser., V. 1977.* The coins are housed in the site museum and have been catalogued by the author.

4. *Caerleon.* The coins are housed in the National Museum of Wales and have been listed there by the author.

5. Bruce-Mitford, J.B. *The Sutton Hoo ship burial. Vol. I The coins by J.P.C. Kent* (1975)

6. Ravetz, A. 'The fourth-century inflation and Roman–British coin finds' *Num. Chron.*, 7th ser., 1964. This seminal paper was the first to establish the principles of like-with-like comparison advocated in this volume.

7. Cunliffe, B.W. *Excavations at Portchester Castle. Vol. 1. Roman* (1975)

8. Thompson, M. *The Athenian agora (loc cit.)*

9. *Vindolanda coins.* The histograms are compiled from the excavations

conducted by R. Birley in the vicus (forthcoming) and by P. Bidwell in the fort itself (forthcoming) as well as from coins from pre-war excavations, museum collections and casual finds. They have been catalogued by the author.

10. Birley, R. *Vindolanda: a Roman frontier post on Hadrian's Wall and its people* (1977)

11. *Usk fortress*. The unpublished details of the Usk excavation are cited with the kind consent of Professor W. Manning. The work on the coins and pottery distribution is the work of Dr Kevin Greene and the interpretation of the context as a commercial centre is that of the author.

12. C.I.L. VIII, 18224. I owe this reference to the kindness of Mark Hassal of London University.

13. The best study of the dating potential is medieval coins, based on hoard evidence and association, is M. Archibald 'English mediaeval coins as dating evidence' in P. J. Casey and R. Reece eds. *Coins and the archaeologist loc cit.*

14. Casey, P. J. *Roman coinage in Britain* 2nd ed. (1983)

15. The coins found with victims of the eruption of Vesuvius are conveniently collected in S. Bolin *State and currency in the Roman empire to 300 AD* (Stockholm, 1954)

16. *Iron Age Coins*. There is an extensive literature on this subject stimulated by the researches of D. F. Allen; the following is a small selection of important books and papers. D. F. Allen 'The origins of coinage in Britan: a reappraisal' in S. S. Frere ed. *Problems of the Iron Age in southern Britain* (1959); D. F. Allen and D. Nash *The coins of the ancient Celts* (1980); D. F. Allen 'The Belgic dynasties of Britain and their coins' *Archaeologia, 90, 1944, 1–46*, and D. Nash 'Settlement and coinage in central Gaul *c*.200–50 BC' (Oxford, 1978). A very extensive bibliography on Celtic coinage will be found in Allen and Nash (Supra)

17. Casey, P. J. 'Roman coinage of the fourth century in Scotland' in R. Miket and C. Burgess eds. *Between the walls: essays on the prehistory and history of the north of Britain in honour of George Jobey (Edinburgh, 1984)*. This analysis is based in the immaculately accurate list of finds of Roman coins found in Scotland published at regular intervals under the auspices of Professor Anne Robertson.

18. Kimes, T. Haselgrove, C. and Hodder, I. 'A method for the identification of regional cultural boundaries' *Jnl. Anthrop. Arch., 1, 113–31*

Chapter 7

1. Sellwood, D. 'Presidential address' *Num. Chron., CXL, 1980, i–vii*

2. Tournaire, J. *et al.* 'Iron Age coin moulds from France' *Procs. Prehist. Soc., 48, 1982, 417–37*

3. Lyon, C. S. S. 'The estimation of the number of dies employed in a coinage' *Num. Circular, 1965, 180–1*

4. Esty, W.W. 'Estimating the size of a coinage' *Num. Chron.*, *144*, *1984*, *180–4*.

5. Crawford, M.J. *Roman republican coinage loc cit.*

6. Sellwood, D. 'Some experiments in Greek minting techniques' *Num. Chron.* 1963, 217–31

7. Kinnes, P. 'The Amphictionic coinage reconsidered' *Num. Chron.*, 1983, 1–22

8. Grierson, P. 'Mint output in the time of Offa' *Num. Circular.*, LXXXI, 1963, 114–5. Also by the same author 'Some aspects of the coinage of Offa' *Num. Circ.*, *LXXXI*, *1963*, *223–5* and 'The volume of Anglo-Saxon coinage' *Econ. Hist. Rev.*, 2nd ser., XX, 1967

9. Carradice, I. *Coinage and finances in the reign of Domitian* (Oxford, 1983)

10. Grierson, P. 'The monetary reforms of 'Abd al-Malik: their metrological basis and their financial repercussions' *Jnl. of the Economic and Social History of the Orient* (Leiden, 1960)

Chapter 8

1. Tanner, B.K. *et al.* 'Ferromagnetism in ancient copper-based coinage' *Nature*, *280*, *5717*, *1979*, *46–8*

2. Cope, L. *The metallurgical development of the Roman Imperial Coinage during the first five centuries A.D.* Unpublished PhD., 1974.

3. Casey, P.J. and Coult, R. 'The Piercebridge (Co. Durham) hoard of mid-third century "antoniniani" and a note on Elmer 593 (Postumus)' *Coin Hoards*, 111, 1977, 72–77

4. Oddy, W.A. *Scientific studies in numismatics* (1980), and Hall, E.T. and Metcalf, D.M. *Methods of chemical and metallurgical investigation of ancient coinage* (1972)

5. Walker, D.R. *The metrology of Roman silver coinage. Vols 1–3* (Oxford, 1976–8)

6. Gordus, A. 'Neutron activation analysis of coins and coin streaks' in Hall, E.T. and Metcalf, D. *loc cit.*

7. Gordus, A. 'Streak analyses' in Hall, E.T. and Metcalf, D. *loc cit.*

8. Gale, N.H. *et al.* 'Mineralogical and geographical silver sources of archaic Greek coinage' in Oddy, W.A. and Metcalf, D. *Metallurgy and numismatics* (1980). In the same publication a sceptical note is sounded from the numismatic quarter in M. Price 'The uses of metal analysis in the study of archaic Greek coinage: some comments'

9. Oddy, W. and Hughes, M. 'The specific gravity method for the analysis of gold coins' in Hall, E.T. and Metcalf, M. *loc cit.*

10. Casey, P.J. and Cronyn, J. *Numismatics and conservation* (Durham, 1980)

Chapter 9

1. Bates, G.E. *Archaeological exploration of Sardis : Byzantine coins* (Harvard, 1971)

Index